MODERN WORLD NATIONS

Pakistan

Second Edition

Samuel Willard Crompton

Series Editor
Charles F. Gritzner
South Dakota State University

An imprint of Infobase Publishing

Frontispiece: Flag of Pakistan

Cover: Muslims gather to pray outside the Badshahi Mosque in Lahore, Pakistan.

Pakistan, Second Edition

Copyright © 2007 by Infobase Publishing

Chelsea House
An imprint of Infobase Publishing
132 West 31st Street
New York NY 10001

Library of Congress Cataloging-in-Publication Data

Crompton, Samuel Willard.
  Pakistan / Samuel Willard Crompton. — 2nd ed.
    p. cm. — (Modern world nations)
  Includes bibliographical references and index.
  ISBN 0-7910-9208-9 (hardcover)
  1. Pakistan—Juvenile literature. I. Title. II. Series.
  DS376.9.C76 2006
  954.91—dc22   2006015642

Chelsea House books are available at special discounts when purchased in bulk quantities for businesses, associations, institutions, or sales promotions. Please call our Special Sales Department in New York at (212) 967-8800 or (800) 322-8755.

You can find Chelsea House on the World Wide Web at http://www.chelseahouse.com

Series and cover design by Takeshi Takahashi

Printed in the United States of America

Bang Hermitage 10 9 8 7 6 5 4 3 2 1

This book is printed on acid-free paper.

All links and Web addresses were checked and verified to be correct at the time of publication. Because of the dynamic nature of the Web, some addresses and links may have changed since publication and may no longer be valid.

Table of Contents

Pakistan

Second Edition

CHAPTER

1

Introducing Pakistan

Pakistan is one of the world's most strategically located countries. Sharing borders with India to the east and south, China to the northeast, Afghanistan to the north and west, and Iran to the west, Pakistan sits at one of the great crossroads of history. Many conquerors and would-be conquerors have traveled through this land, and many an army has struggled through the mountains of Pakistan and delighted in the open floodplains of the Indus River. But no one conqueror has ever fully gained control over Pakistan. This can be attributed in part to the country's diverse lands and peoples but also to the large number of foreign conquerors who have struggled to gain ascendancy.

In many ways, Pakistan is a nation still in search of its identity. Though the modern state was created in 1947, Pakistanis still feel insecure about their place in the world. This insecurity is bred partly by the circumstance of history, and partly because of its gigantic

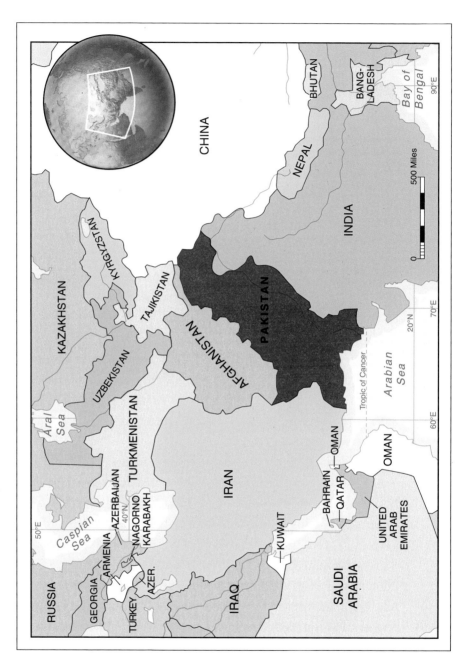

Pakistan was established as a modern state in 1947, when it was partitioned from British-controlled India. The nation shares borders with India to the east and south, China to the northeast, Afghanistan to the west and north, and Iran to the west.

neighbor to the southeast, India. Pakistan and India were created within 24 hours of each other, but the two nations are not on friendly terms. In fact, they have fought three wars against one another since the partition of the two countries in August 1947. And today, both countries are armed with nuclear weapons.

For many Americans, their first real awareness of Pakistan came with the tragic events of September 11, 2001. Until then, Pakistan had been a distant, shadowy presence that few Americans other than important policymakers cared much about. But this lack of interest changed abruptly after hijacked airplanes crashed into the World Trade Center, the Pentagon, and a field in Pennsylvania. After these events, Americans suddenly became more aware of and interested in Pakistan, as well as its neighbor to the north and west, Afghanistan.

THE WAR ON TERROR

On the morning of September 11, 2001, no one could have predicted that the day's events would suddenly change much of the world. The United States was at peace, as was Pakistan. The cold war between the Soviet Union and the United States had ended nearly a decade earlier. Major world nations were still discussing how to apportion the "peace dividend" that came as a result of having to spend less money on military arsenals.

Yet that morning, four American airplanes were hijacked. Two crashed into New York's spectacular twin towers of the World Trade Center, a third inflicted damage on the Pentagon in Washington, D.C., and a fourth crashed in rural Pennsylvania, killing all those onboard (rather than those individuals at its intended target, the White House). Approximately 3,000 Americans were killed in lower Manhattan, while loss of life at the Pentagon was relatively small.

Almost at once, American president George W. Bush seized the initiative. He declared a new war—the War on Terror—a conflict that was not contained by national boundaries. The president declared the United States would make no distinction between those governments that sponsored terrorism and those that sheltered terrorists. A new world era had begun.

Where did Pakistan stand? The country and its leaders had been friendly to the Taliban government in Afghanistan. But Pakistan also relied on U.S. economic assistance, which would clearly be withdrawn if Pakistan did not back the United States in the new War on Terror. President Pervez Musharraf made his decision very quickly: Pakistan would stand with the United States.

Many books have been written about Pakistan since September 11, 2001, but none have managed to fully unravel the riddle of that nation. Even more than Afghanistan, which has a firmly Muslim identity, and even more than India, which has a strong Hindu identity, Pakistan was created from several competing identities.

CONTEMPORARY CONCERNS

In today's Pakistan, there are many issues that define the nation. First and foremost is the Pakistani military. Since 1947, the year that India and Pakistan were partitioned, the Pakistani military has governed the nation through at least half of its history. There have been several military dictators, and at times it seems that only a firm military presence can hold this diverse and in many ways divergent nation together. Of course this does not mean that Pakistanis are not in favor of democracy; many of them fight for democratic reforms. But even those who yearn for democracy know that Pakistan is built on a set of difficult compromises between church and state, Hindu and Muslim, and urban versus rural.

Second, identity is closely identified with the Islamic faith. One can debate whether *Islam* or *Muslim* is the better term. Both words mean adhering to the word of Allah. But the world of Islam stretches over thousands of miles, between West Africa and Indonesia, whereas Muslim refers to the individual members of the faith. The Muslim faith came to Pakistan in the eighth century A.D. The Prophet Muhammad had his religious visions and revelations during the seventh century, and after his death his followers began to spread the faith. Conquering Muslim warriors came to Pakistan and established a number of Islamic states that flourished on the subcontinent. There was no separation between Pakistan and India at that time; the two formed separate parts of a larger geographical whole.

Today, Pakistan is about 95 percent Muslim, with small minorities of Hindu, Farsee, and other faiths. Pakistan is officially an Islamic state, but according to the Pakistani Constitution, church and state are separate. This makes Pakistan a more attractive ally for Western countries such as Great Britain and the United States.

One of the least mentioned conflicts is the intense rivalry between rural Pakistanis and those living in the country's cities. Until about a century ago, Pakistanis were an overwhelmingly rural people. They irrigated and farmed the lands around the Indus River, creating one of the miracles of modern-day agriculture. During the nineteenth century, the British government of Queen Victoria, which ruled the entire Indian subcontinent, helped make Pakistan a breadbasket.

The twentieth century brought great changes, especially in terms of migration from the country to the city. Pakistan has eight cities with populations exceeding one million people. Its largest urban center, Karachi, is home to an estimated 12 to 14 million residents! This mass exodus from the countryside to cities has occurred on a much larger scale than the rural-to-urban migration the United States experienced during the nineteenth century. The massive shift in population, as might be expected, has been accompanied by a great number of complex social and economic problems. Several of Pakistan's major cities, including Karachi, simply cannot accommodate so many people. Some surveys place Karachi at the very bottom among the world's cities in terms of poverty, pollution, and rampant crime.

Considering its sharp divisions in religion, military bureaucracy versus desire for democracy, and patterns of settlement (where people live), it would be quite easy to believe that Pakistan would unravel as a state. Yet, this has not occurred. The country has survived reasonably well for some six decades and there is reason to believe that it will continue to thrive as an independent state. The larger and in many ways more important question is whether Pakistan can coexist with its neighbor India. Also of concern is whether the country can find a middle road between Western capitalist nations and Asian socialist ones.

THE 2005 EARTHQUAKE

The events of September 11, 2001, helped make Pakistan somewhat more visible to Americans and other Westerners. But another event, that of October 8, 2005, made the plight of Pakistan and other Third World countries much more obvious to the West. Around 9:00 A.M. on that date, a massive earthquake—registering 7.6 on the Richter scale—struck the northeast section of Pakistan. The quake came just as children were starting into their school day, and thousands of young people were crushed to death at the very beginning of the tragedy. The quake's center was about 60 miles (100 kilometers) northeast of Islamabad, threatening the country's capital and the very nerve center of the Pakistani nation.

Help was immediately rushed to the northeast section of the country, but in many locations it arrived too late. Much of the country's communications and transportation infrastructure were damaged or destroyed. Soldiers and rescue workers were slow to arrive and the emergency relief effort was poorly coordinated. Many people were buried alive beneath rubble, but by the time they were reached, it was too late to dig them out. There were, however, some miraculous stories. Rescue workers occasionally found young boys and girls who were trapped as long as four or five days, placing them at the extreme

On October 8, 2005, a massive earthquake hit northern Pakistan, killing more than 87,000 people and leaving more than 3 million others homeless. Pictured here are three girls playing in the streets of Muzaffarabad, Pakistan, a couple of weeks after the earthquake, which measured 7.6 on the Richter scale.

upper limit of human survival. But for every boy or girl who was rescued, at least a dozen and perhaps as many as 20 others perished in the schoolyards, leaving their parents in enormous distress. News services around the world lamented the loss of an entire generation of young people in some sections of Pakistan.

As days and weeks passed after the quake, the tragic results became more apparent. More than 87,000 people perished in the earthquake itself and another 3 million were made homeless. This tragedy was on such an immense scale that it could only be compared to the tragic tsunami in the Indian Ocean nine months earlier.

International organizations such as the Red Cross are widely respected for coming to the rescue of people in times of need, and Pakistan was no exception. Large numbers of rescue workers came from faraway countries, and large amounts of money was raised. But no matter how much was done, it was not enough. No outside assistance could make up for the immense human dislocation and widespread suffering caused by this earthquake. Unfortunately, the United States was preoccupied at this critical time, because it, too, was suffering from its own natural disaster—Hurricane Katrina and the widespread destruction it caused in New Orleans and elsewhere along the Gulf Coast. As a result, the United States had less money to offer Pakistanis as they began their road to recovery.

It will take years, if not decades, for Pakistan to recover from the devastating earthquake of 2005. The national government, which had managed to survive several years of a somewhat shaky alliance with the United States in the War on Terror, was now confronted with one of the great modern tragedies. Worst of all, winter was descending into the foothills of the Himalayan Mountains.

Human beings are very resourceful, and it is likely that Pakistan will weather this storm as it has so many others. But the earthquake of 2005 showed both the fragility of the Pakistani nation, and the fundamental truth that nature always has the last word. Let us now turn our attention to the ways in which nature has shaped Pakistan.

2

Physical Landscapes

In her 1975 book, *The Lion River: The Indus*, author Jean Fairley writes of the Indus River: "Of all these names the first seems to me the most apt, for the Indus is a lion throughout its course. It is beautiful, powerful, unpredictable and dangerous . . . Both in time and space, the Indus is cruel and as ruthless and cunning as any lion." This is an apt description of one of the earth's most important rivers, because though people's lives are primarily spent on the land, their sustenance is often drawn from the earth's many waterways. This is certainly true in Pakistan, a country where 75 percent of the land would not be arable without the use of irrigation.

THE INDUS

The country's lifeblood, the Indus River stretches nearly 2,000 miles (more than 3,200 kilometers) from headwaters to mouth, and passes through terrain that is rugged and difficult to traverse. Because our

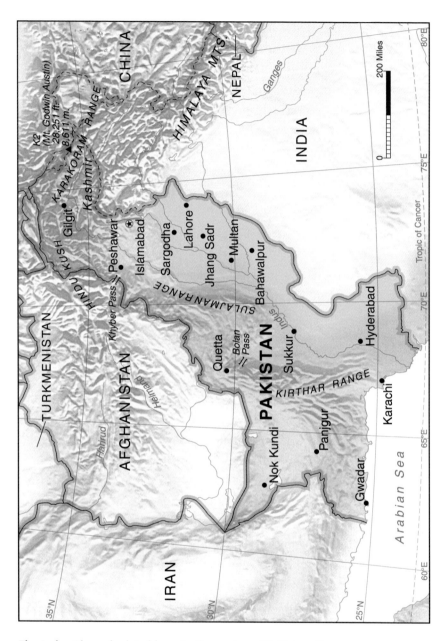

The Indus River, depicted here in the center of Pakistan, flows some 1,988 miles (3,200 kilometers) from its source in Tibet to its mouth at the Arabian Sea, near the city of Karachi. The Indus is the key component to Pakistan's economy; it supplies water for agricultural production and supports many heavy industries.

geographic attention is focused elsewhere, perhaps the Indus River is not as well known to many Northern Americans as are such waterways as the Nile, Tigris, Euphrates, or Amazon. Even so, the Indus is a giant among the world's rivers, ranking among the largest in terms of length, volume, and importance to the parched land across which it flows during its lower course. The Indus has given life to thriving civilizations, including present-day Pakistan, for more than 4,000 years. Even the name of the entire subcontinent—India—is derived from Indus. For these and other reasons, it is vital to learn about the Indus River if one is to understand Pakistan—past and present.

The Indus has had many names given to it by fishermen, tradesmen, villagers, and peasants throughout the centuries, or even millennia. One of the most appropriate names was given by the Tibetan people who live near the river's source: Father Indus, the Lion River.

No Westerner saw the upper reaches of the Indus until hardy Portuguese priests visited the headwaters region in the seventeenth century. The priests wrote a report that made the countryside sound dismal and depressing—perhaps because they wanted to discourage other Europeans from visiting. As a result, it was not until 1907 that the first European—Sven Hedin—finally visited the source of the Indus.

Hedin, a Swedish-born explorer, first traveled north to Lake Manasarowar in Tibet. There, he was told by local people that the lake was the source for four great rivers: the Brahmaputra, Indus, Ganges, and Sutlej. Hedin felt confident the lake was not the source of the Indus, but he began his explorations there anyway. Traveling the lake's waters in an inflatable boat he had brought with him, Hedin confirmed that the lake was not the source of the rivers. He then continued to explore northward. He went first to Mount Kalias, a towering 22,000-foot (6,706 meter-) peak that is the inspiration for many Tibetan traditions. About 30 miles (48 kilometers) north of Mount Kalias and 80 miles (129 kilometers) north of Lake Manasarowar, he found "an insignificant stream," and then a "tiny brook" at about 17,000 feet (5,182 meters) above sea level flowing from a glaciated hillside. Hedin, who had a sense of the dramatic, wrote, "Here I stood and saw the Indus emerge from the lap of the earth." The natives call the spot Hedin described *Singi Kabab*, which means "the Mouth of the Lion."

Some people still debate whether Hedin found the exact spot. There are hundreds, if not thousands, of springs and brooks that feed into the Indus. It is possible another one may be found someday that is longer and more central to the river than Hedin's discovery. In any event, Hedin estimated the source for the Indus, which gives life to the dry and dusty lands of Pakistan. It is difficult for Westerners to reach the source today, because it lies within Tibet, which is controlled by the People's Republic of China.

By accepting Hedin's source, the description of the Indus can be narrowed down to this: It rises in Tibet; it runs through mountain gorges with the Himalayas to its south and the Karakorum range to its north; it descends from 17,000 to 5,000 feet (5,182 to 1,524 meters) above sea level as it crosses the northern tip of India; it then makes a sharp left turn, and heads to the plains of Pakistan; from there, it ultimately finds its way to the Arabian Sea.

Rising in western Tibet, the Indus runs on a course due west for some time. In its first 500 miles (805 kilometers), the river drops 12,000 feet (3,658 meters)—from 17,000 feet (5,182 meters) above sea level to about 5,000 feet (1,524 meters). As the gap between the Himalayas to the south and the Karakorum to the north narrows, the Indus becomes a churning, angry river, seeking to break through the rock that confines it. It winds its way through the Indian province of Ladakh and on into Kashmir's Baltistan Province, before taking a short, but sharp turn to the south.

As the Indus resumes its westward course, on its left (southern) bank one can see Nanga Parbat, 26,000 feet (7,925 meters) high and one of the most impressive mountains in the world. This was the mountain that the German climber Heinrich Harrer wanted to scale in 1939. He set off for it, but was detained by the British at the beginning of World War II. Harrer escaped captivity, and went over the Himalayas into Tibet, where he spent time with the young Dalai Lama, Tenzin Gyatso. Harrer's account, *Seven Years in Tibet*, is a masterpiece of adventure literature and was made into a film in 1997.

Harrer did not conquer Nanga Parbat; in fact, no one did until 1953, the same year that Edmund Hillary and Tensing Norgay climbed Mount Everest. The forbidding mountain still looms over the Indus River.

About 75 miles (121 kilometers) past Nanga Parbat, the Indus turns south again. There is no alternative. The Hindu Kush Mountains lie directly ahead, so the river is forced to turn south and enter the alluvial plains that make up the bulk of Pakistan.

The Indus River emerges from the mountains onto the Potwar Plateau, which ranges between 1,000 and 2,000 feet (305 to 610 meters) above sea level. Almost at once, the Indus encounters a new obstacle—a great dam at Tarbela. Built between 1968 and 1976, the dam stands 469 feet (143 meters) high and is 2,264 feet (690 meters) thick at the base. Along with the Mangla Dam on the Chenab River, the Tarbela Dam makes irrigation possible for the entire region of the Punjab, which lies just below it.

The Northwest Frontier Province and the Khyber Pass

The Northwest Frontier Province (NWFP) lies on the right bank as the Indus descends from the mountains to the plains. As a traveler leaves the Indus and heads west, he or she moves steadily uphill to the NWFP, also known as the land of the Pathans (or Pashtuns).

Through the centuries, the Khyber Pass has been a gateway to the Indian subcontinent, and today many smugglers use the 40-mile-long pass to transport goods into Pakistan. Many types of contraband, such as electronics and textiles, are smuggled from Afghanistan to Pakistan, where they are often sold cheaply in Peshawar, Lahore, and Karachi.

This is a landscape as rich in imagery as it has been in historic confrontations between peoples who wanted to secure the mountain passes. The Northwest Frontier Province is the traditional gateway between Afghanistan and Pakistan, and the point of entry to the entire Indian subcontinent.

This is the land in which the "Great Game" was played between British and Russian scouts in the nineteenth century. Both British and Russian adventurers wanted to secure this area for their nations. The Great Game began in the 1840s, when the British entered what is now Pakistan. They defeated the Sikhs in a short and bloody war and proceeded to make central Pakistan a British province. The Northwest Frontier Province was the gateway from that land to Afghanistan, and therefore was like a swinging door: It opened from either end.

The Russians, who had expanded steadily into central Asia since about 1800, were eager to find a way into the Indian sub-continent. The only natural and logical way for them to do so was through the Khyber Pass, which is full of romantic stories, legends, and smugglers, even today. About 40 miles long, the Khyber Pass extends between Peshawar in Pakistan to Kabul in Afghanistan. It is a natural gateway located more than 10,000 feet (3,048 meters) above sea level. Here, Alexander the Great and Babur the Moghul entered the subcontinent. Nineteenth-century Russians intended to follow in the footsteps of their predecessors.

The Russians were thwarted by British scouts and agents who played the Great Game between about 1850 and 1895. In 1897, British Lord Durand undertook a major scouting and surveying expedition. Its result was the Durand Line, drawn between British India and Russian-dominated Afghanistan. The line is still the official border today. It separates the Pathans (Pashtuns), half of whom are in Afghanistan and half of whom are in Pakistan. This division has led to calls for a new country to be created called Pashtunistan.

A recent description of the Khyber Pass was made by Stephen Alter, an Indian of American descent, in his book *Amritsar to Lahore: A Journey Across the India-Pakistan Border*:

> In essence a road provides access to trade and territory while a border restricts movement along that route. The intersection of these two lines on a map represents specific points of conflict. Nowhere in the world is this more evident than along the mountainous frontier of Pakistan and Afghanistan. The history of South Asia has long been dictated by the accessibility of routes across the Hindu Kush and the generally unsuccessful lines of defense that were put up to block invaders and regulate trade.

The Khyber Pass is frequented today by smugglers carrying goods on bicycles. They race up and down the dangerous road to bring goods from one country to another. To them, the land is all the same; most of them belong to the tribe of Pashtuns who have long controlled this mountainous terrain. For a true foreigner, the boundaries are obvious. As Stephen Alter wrote:

> Two kilometers beyond Landi Kotal we came to a place called Michni Kandao. Here there was a signboard that read, "Foreigners are not permitted beyond this point." Though the mountains were obscured by a haze of dust, I could see just across into Afghanistan. The entire landscape was a khaki brown, except for the brightly painted buses, with bulging sides, that carried passengers to Torkham.

The Punjab

Leaving the Northwest Frontier Province and returning to the Indus River, travellers next enter the Punjab (Land of Five Rivers), which stands on the river's left (eastern) bank. The Punjab is made by the movement and eventual meeting of five rivers. Moving from east to west (from right to left on a map), they are the Jhelum, Chenab, Ravi, Beas, and Sutlej. The rivers join in the lower Punjab and form the last stretch of the mighty Indus River. One of the few solid agreements made between Pakistan and India concerns these rivers. Under the Waters Treaty of 1960, it was agreed that India would have exclusive use of the waters of the three easternmost rivers, and that Pakistan would have exclusive use of the Jhelum and Indus. So far this agreement has worked well for both nations.

Despite the great flow of waters, much of the area between the rivers was dry and arid until the British began irrigation projects around 1850. Since then, the Punjab has become the breadbasket for most of Pakistan. Cotton, jute, rice, millet, and other crops are produced there in great quantities.

The Grand Trunk Road slices neatly through the Punjab, beginning at Lahore, and making its way to Peshawar. This bisection from east to west parallels the more profound bisection that occurred when Pakistan and India were created. The Punjab was split between the two countries. Pakistan received about 63 percent of the land and a greater percentage of its people. Millions of people were affected by the event, and bitterness still exists on both sides of the border.

The dislocations caused by the separation are painful and have had long-lasting consequences. Because of the distrust and suspicion between India and Pakistan, a simple border crossing from Lahore in Pakistan to Amritsar in India can take about 15 hours. Stephen Alter chronicled his crossing in 1997:

> The temperature had been climbing since morning and it was now past noon, the air thick with humidity and flies. I found a place to sit down, next to the fence, which gave me a view of the custom's inspectors on the other side. For the next three hours I watched the lines move slowly forward as the officials put each traveler through an inquisition. There was something vindictive in the way they treated the passengers, as if these were traitors or enemies of the state simply because they were crossing the border.

Whether they live in Pakistan or in India, many people of the Punjab area simply call themselves "Punjabis," which was their geographic name long before the two nations were created in 1947. Although anxiety and tension exist at nearly every place along the border between Pakistan and India, it is most pronounced in the Punjab, where the natural landscape was cut in half in an attempt to find a solution to religious tensions.

The Land of Five Rivers may sound like a well-watered, harmonious place, but without irrigation, half of it would be a desert. The heat is intense and the mixture of dust and humidity can overwhelm even the strongest workers. Dams are vital to the well-being of the Punjab, which is the political and cultural center of Pakistan.

Many forces are at work throughout the landscape. Pakistan is rarely harmonious—or bland. Instead, it is a land—and a country—of remarkable contrasts.

Baluchistan

As one travels farther south along the Indus, the landscape divides into the province of Baluchistan on the west bank and the province of Sind on the east bank. Baluchistan is the least populous part of the country. It contains about 40 percent of Pakistan's land, but only about 4 percent of the people live there. It is a hard, dusty landscape that few foreigners have seen. Alexander the Great and his army nearly perished here in 323 B.C., when they left the Indus and headed to Baluchistan on their way to Persia. Of the many images of Alexander the Great, one of the most popular shows the Macedonian conqueror receiving a helmet of water collected by his followers. Urged to drink the water to keep his strength, Alexander poured the precious liquid out in the desert to show he would share the hardships with his men. Alexander and his men did reach Persia, but few conquerors since have chosen the same route.

Baluchistan remains the most undeveloped part of Pakistan. Tribal peoples weave cloth the same way they did 1,000 years ago, and make a meager living by moving their herds from south to north during the summer months. Still, Baluchistan often inspires admiration among the people who see it. Historian Arnold J. Toynbee wrote: "Have you ever doubted Man's heroism? If you have, plunge southward from Quetta into Central Baluchistan, and your doubts will have been dispelled long before you have reached Khuzdar."

This is some of the most desolate landscape on the face of the earth. Few rivers flow through Baluchistan. Camels and packhorses find occasional oases, but there is very little true relief from the parched conditions. This is not a dramatic desert of sand, like those found in Saudi Arabia, but a hard, dry land surface that receives only about five inches (13 centimeters) of rainfall per year. Sand columns abound, and travelers have often commented that Baluchistan closely resembles the moon.

This is where the Indus flows into the Arabian Sea. Along its journey of 1,988 miles (3,200 kilometers) from the mountains of Tibet, the Indus generates 3 times as much flow as the Nile, and 10 times as much as the Colorado River in the American Southwest. Today, the mighty Indus displays less of its former magnificence because of the large number of dams upstream and the diversion of water for irrigation.

Even with its reduced current and flow, the Indus still has about four branches that empty into the Arabian Sea, creating a delta that rivals the Lena Delta in Siberia and the Mississippi Delta south of New Orleans. Like those other deltas, the Indus River Delta has branches that change their course periodically. In fact, shifting deltas explain why the once great town of Bambhore is small today, whereas Karachi, which is located on one of the river's several distributaries, has grown to be a huge metropolis.

Located just west of the Indus Delta, Karachi is an enormous port city. Just 150 years ago, it was a small town, and even by 1947, it had only 400,000 inhabitants. Today, it has between 12 and 14 million people, and is one of the most troubled places on the subcontinent, if not the world. The gap between rich and poor is especially evident in Karachi. Upper-class businessmen live in homes that resemble forts, while hundreds of thousands of unemployed people roam the streets, occasionally holding large demonstrations. It is perhaps fortunate for government officials that the Pakistani capital was moved north to Islamabad in 1962. The move gave an impression of abandonment, as if Karachi's problems are too great to be solved.

As a port city, Karachi is as important to Pakistan as New York City, San Francisco, and New Orleans combined are to the United States. Karachi's influence reaches far upstream, as it is

Over the last 50 years, Karachi has grown into one of the largest cities in the world. Unfortunately, with this rapid growth has come excessive poverty; nearly half of the country's population live in illegal slum dwellings, which have neither running water or sewage disposal.

also the major port for Afghanistan. However, Karachi is not a popular tourist destination. Foreigners use its excellent airport and then quickly depart for other parts of the country.

East and north of Karachi are the ruins of Mohenjo-daro, the site of one of the world's oldest civilizations. Tourists can see the mud-dried bricks that supported a city of perhaps 50,000 people between 2500 and 1700 B.C. It is not known exactly what happened to Mohenjo-daro. For generations, it was believed that this early civilization was wiped out by Indo-Aryans who migrated from the north. It is just as possible, however, that Mohenjo-daro fell victim to the shifting waters of the Indus.

Sind

East of Mohenjo-daro and east of the Indus River lies the province of Sind. It is an arid landscape that has been partially transformed by a major dam upstream at Sukhor. Even so, Sind is one of the least hospitable areas of Pakistan to foreigners, and it is the place where tribal and village lords hold the most power. Though there are democratic elections throughout Pakistan, it is well known that villagers cannot vote against the wishes of their landlords in the Sind.

Finally, the Indus, in more than half a dozen shallow channels, meets the Arabian Sea. It is a magical spot, but also a lonely one. Like the tiny spring where it begins, the Indus comes to an end in a remote area. The extremely flat Indus River Delta is one of the world's largest, occupying an area of 3,000 square miles (4,828 square kilometers). In the delta, there are small fishing boats and people searching the water for crabs. Generally speaking, however, not many people inhabit the area. In this respect, it resembles the all but inaccessible mouth of the Colorado River as it flows into the Gulf of California, or the sparsely populated delta region of the Mississippi River below New Orleans.

The Indus moves about one million tons of silt a day, and that silt has been piling up in the delta for thousands of years. The coast today is between 50 and 80 miles (80 and 129 kilometers) farther south than it was 2,000 years ago, and the silt keeps piling up.

Beyond the silt and coast lies the Arabian Sea, which was once known as the Sea of Sinbad. For at least 20 miles (32 kilometers) out, the grayish-green of the river mixes with the blue-green of the sea. Perhaps it is fitting that the Indus begins in a place of mystery, near Mount Kalias, and ends on a lonely coastal spot that summons up images from a bygone age. At least half of the great Lion River remains a mystery, even to those who have spent a lifetime beside it.

3

Pakistan, The Land of the Pure

Muhammad Iqbal (1877–1938) was an Indian Muslim philosopher and poet who was inspired with a vision of a new world, one influenced both by the age-old history of the Indian subcontinent and by Islam, the faith of the Prophet Muhammad. In numerous poems, Iqbal urged his fellow Muslims to rise and become a great force in the world, as was their destiny. One of Iqbal's poems was "To the Panjab Peasant":

What is this life of yours, tell me its mystery—
Trampled in dust is your ages-old history!
Deep in that dust has been smothered your flame—
Wake, and hear dawn its high summons proclaim!
Creatures of dust from the soil may draw bread:
Not in that darkness is Life's river fed!
Base will his metal be held, who on earth

Put not to trial his innermost worth!
Break all the idols of tribe and of caste,
Break the old customs that fetter men fast!
Here is true victory, here is faith's crown—
One creed and one world, division thrown down!
Cast on the soil of your clay the heart's seed:
Promise of harvest to come is that seed!

Iqbal wrote this poem early in the twentieth century. The Panjab (or Punjab) peasant was indeed "trampled in dust" at that time. The Punjab is the heart of Pakistan today, but around the turn of the twentieth century, it was a provincial backwater, valued by the British conquerors only for its wheat and its

Today, the Punjab region is the center of Pakistan's agricultural economy, but more than 100 hundred years ago it was considered a provincial backwater. This lithograph painted by Charles Hardinge, who served as viceroy of India from 1910 to 1916, depicts a remote Punjabi city at the base of the Himalaya Mountains.

proximity to the mountain passes that led to neighboring Afghanistan. The British, and perhaps many of the Punjabis themselves, had forgotten that a long, tumultuous, and glorious history lay in the dust of the Punjab: Alexander the Great walked there, the teachings of Buddha and the Indian mystic Kabir had been preached there, and Islam had been carried there by Turkish warriors a thousand years earlier. Much of this was forgotten. Iqbal spoke truly when he wrote, "Deep in that dust has been smothered your flame."

PUNJAB UNDER BRITISH RULE

Iqbal felt passionate about the Punjab. He was born there, at Sialkot, in 1877. First educated in Lahore, he went to England and studied both at Cambridge and at a German university between 1905 and 1908. He received his doctorate and was even knighted by the British government in 1922, but his deepest allegiance was to the Punjab.

Iqbal referred to the Punjab as it was—the breadbasket of British-ruled India. The British had begun a series of canals and irrigation projects around 1850, and the result was that the Punjab, already known for the quality of its crops, now began to produce those crops in much larger quantities. Punjabi irrigation was viewed as one of the outstanding achievements of the British Empire, a testament to the beneficent influence of British rule. But Iqbal saw it differently, commenting that, "Not in that darkness is Life's river fed!"

During his years in England and Germany, Iqbal had become well acquainted with the major philosophers of the day. He first learned, and then rejected the major teachings of the European philosophers. Iqbal came to believe that Europe and the West were in a state of moral and intellectual decline. Rejuvenation would not come from European cities, argued Iqbal. It would come from a resurgence of Eastern peoples, informed both by their magnificent histories and by the Muslim faith. In 1930, he became president of the Muslim League, a religious and political organization devoted to finding a new way of life for the Muslim peoples of the subcontinent.

Iqbal believed that the Eastern peoples—those of the Indian subcontinent in particular—were held back by customs that had developed over the past 3,000 years: those of tribe and of caste.

TRADITION AND CASTE

Caste is a Portuguese word that came to India in the sixteenth century, but it refers to a social ranking that has governed life on the subcontinent for millennia. The caste system differentiated and discriminated among the people of India. A person was born into a certain caste and remained there. There was no concept of self-improvement leading to social advancement. One was what one was born to be.

A tribe is the furthest extension of family loyalty. Tribal customs and loyalty shape people's minds and hearts more deeply than nationality. Tribal loyalties were especially strong in British India, and Iqbal saw these as part of the formula that kept the Indian peoples from attaining the glory they deserved. Pakistanis today remain a strongly tribal people, and the Pashtuns—who live on the border between Pakistan and Afghanistan—are the largest autonomous tribal group on Earth.

Iqbal spelled out his answer to these dilemmas of tribe and caste in his poetry:

Here is true victory, here is faith's crown—
One creed and one world, division thrown down!
Cast on the soil of your clay the heart's seed:
Promise of harvest to come is that seed!

"One creed and one world" meant that Islam would be triumphant. Iqbal was not a militaristic or vainglorious man, but he clearly believed that the Muslim faith was the best the world had to offer, and that it should spread everywhere. When he

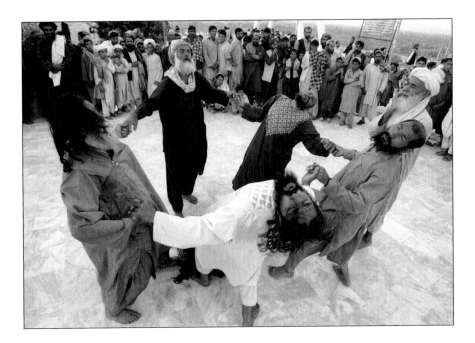

The Pashtuns, who live in the border region of Afghanistan and Pakistan, are the largest autonomous tribal group on Earth. More than 28 million Pashtuns live in Pakistan, and the group is known for its devotion to Islam and its strict code of honor.

referred to "division thrown down!" Iqbal probably meant British India, in which millions of people divided by tribe and caste were easily ruled by a small number of English soldiers and administrators.

LAND OF THE PURE

During the 1930s, a group of Indian students at Cambridge University in England designed an acronym for the country that Iqbal envisioned. They put together eight letters:

P-A-K-I-S-T-A-N. In Urdu, the language of the educated classes, the word means "Land of the Pure," but it also stands for some of the land and landscape of the country. The "P" stands for Punjab; the "A" stands for Afghan; the "K" stands for Kashmir (which is now divided between Pakistan and India);

and the "STAN" is for Baluchistan. This acronym, created around 1933, has become the name of the country that was carved out of Iqbal's vision and the political compromises that followed the British departure from the subcontinent in 1947.

Iqbal died in 1938, just nine years before the Indian subcontinent was released from British rule. Two nations rather than one emerged: India and Pakistan. Iqbal's beliefs helped create the nation of Pakistan, the "Land of the Pure."

4

Pakistan Through Time

F ew countries have weathered as many changes in government, religion, and society as has Pakistan. From the days of the Indus Valley civilization to the modern-day Islamic Republic of Pakistan, the land and its people have undergone change time and again. A short list of governments and dynasties follows:

Indus Valley civilization: 2500–1700 B.C.
Vedic Period: 1700–600 B.C.
States: 300 B.C.–A.D. 300
Fragmentation: A.D. 300–1000
Delhi Sultanate: 1250–1526
Moghul Dynasty: 1526–1760
Warring States: 1760–1860
British Raj: 1860–1947
Republic of Pakistan: 1947–present

To this list must be added a second to illustrate the appearance and development of different religions in Pakistan.

Tribal, Pantheistic: Prehistoric
Polytheistic, formal: 2500–1700 B.C.
Vedic, Aryan: 1600 B.C.
Buddhist and Jain: 600 B.C.
Christianity: First century A.D.
Muslim: Eighth century A.D.
Sikh: Fifteenth century A.D.
Kabir: Fifteenth century A.D.

Future archaeological digs may prove current theories wrong, but most experts believe that civilization began in Pakistan around 2500 B.C. Pakistan was one of the three early "cradles of civilization." The other two were in Egypt, centered on the Nile River, and in Mesopotamia, centered between the Tigris and Euphrates rivers. For centuries, students of history considered these two the major cradles of civilization until a series of archaeological digs conducted in the 1920s indicated that there was a third cradle along the banks of the Indus River in what is now Pakistan.

INDUS VALLEY CIVILIZATION

Sometime around 2500 B.C., a civilization arose that was centered in about half a dozen cities sprinkled from the Punjab to the middle of the Sind. All these cities had populations of around 25,000 to 30,000, but the best preserved sites and the ones that have yielded the most to archaeologists are Mohenjo-daro in the Sind and Harappa in the Punjab. Even though more sites have been discovered in Mohenjo-daro, scholars tend to call this early civilization either "Harappan" or "Indus Valley civilization."

The Harappans, as the entire civilization was called, employed advanced building and irrigation techniques.

Located in the Sind region of Pakistan, Mohenjo-daro is one of two (along with Harappa) Indus Valley civilization sites that have been preserved to the present day. Built around 3000 B.C., the site was rediscovered by archaeologists in the 1920s.

Mud-dried bricks (*adobe* in Spanish) were put together to make houses, apartments, and towns, and canals were dug to make good use of the waters of the Indus River. Some scholars suggest that the Harappans achieved a level of comfort, for the upper class at least, that exceeded the living standards of many people in India and Pakistan today.

The Harappans used a written script, but it has never been deciphered. It bears no resemblance to the languages used in Egypt or Mesopotamia. About all that scholars have been able to decipher are the seals that are in pictographic form. They usually show animals and trade goods. This meager evidence suggests that the Harappans were a merchant-oriented people, and they may have been the eastern extension of a trade network that reached at least as far as Mesopotamia (present-day Iraq). Until the Harappan script is deciphered, a certain amount of guess-work is required to figure out what happened to the Harappans and the Indus Valley civilization.

The Indus Valley civilization declined after about 2000 B.C. and virtually disappeared after about 1700 B.C. How and why this happened has been the subject of scholarly debate for at least 50 years. There are two scenarios that are considered most likely, although the reason may in fact be a combination of the two, or some other theory that may soon arise.

First is the Aryan invasion theory. There is no doubt that there was a group of tribal peoples collectively called "Aryan," and that they entered what is now Pakistan between about 2000 and 1500 B.C. The Aryans came from the steppes of central Asia, and they entered Pakistan with new animals—sheep, horses, cattle—and new weapons made of bronze, which allowed them to first invade, and then dominate the local peoples. Whether the Aryans actually conquered the cities of the Indus River valley, or whether those cities suffered from a long, slow decline is uncertain. What is certain is that the cities were practically abandoned by about 1700 B.C.

The second theory is that the Indus River changed its course enough times, and to such a significant degree, that the cities of the Harappan civilization fell when they lost their water supplies.

The next 1,000 years belong to a period known as "Vedic," or "Brahmanic." The Vedic and Brahmanic texts come from an oral tradition that developed between about 1500 and 500 B.C., and much of the Hindu religion comes from these early beginnings. The scene and site of civilization shifted away from Pakistan during this period and was concentrated on the Gangetic Plain—the lands around the Ganges River in central and eastern India. Pakistan was an isolated place during this period, but it remained—and always will remain—important because of its position at the western door to the Indian subcontinent.

During the Vedic era, social divisions among the subcontinent's people became firmer. Although the word *caste* did not come until later, Indians (people of the subcontinent) began to be divided between Brahmans (priests), Kshatriyas (warriors), Vaishyas (merchants), and Sudras (serfs). It is likely that the lighter-skinned Aryans occupied the top two castes and that the darker-skinned original inhabitants made up the two lower castes. The specific rules and regulations of each caste group became more defined. Nothing was more insulting to an Indian than to suggest that he or she perform work that was not appropriate to his or her caste. Pakistan today is a caste-free society, although the Republic of India has retained many of the social ranks.

BUDDHISM AND JAINISM

Perhaps in response to Brahmanic culture and the development of the caste system, two major new religions were founded in India during the sixth century B.C. Buddhism developed through the life and teachings of Siddhartha Gautama, later known as the Buddha. Born into a warrior caste in northern India, Siddhartha enjoyed a life of pleasure and ease until the age of 29. At that time, he voluntarily renounced his position to spend years searching for enlightenment, or "spiritual truth." After many years of apparently unsuccessful searching, Siddhartha attained enlightenment as he sat under a tree. He came to the decision, or realization, that all of life is suffering, and that the only cure for life's suffering is nonattachment: to avoid becoming attached to any person, place, or thing. Desire, in other words, is the cause of all suffering.

Known to his followers as the Buddha, the Enlightened One, Siddhartha traveled and taught for the rest of his life. His teachings are encompassed in the Eight-Fold Path, which includes concepts such as right thought, right action, right livelihood, and right speech. The Buddha's teachings took root in what is now India, and spread to Pakistan, Tibet, Burma, and eventually, to

China. Everywhere the Buddhist faith travels, it brings with it the dual message of compassion and nonattachment.

Mahavira may have been a contemporary of the Buddha. Mahavira believed in many of the principles taught by the Buddha, but went further in relation to the concept of nonviolence. Mahavira expanded nonviolence to mean noninjury to every living thing, including flies, worms, and insects. Many scholars have pointed out the negative implications of Mahavira's beliefs: If worms and insects cannot be harmed, then how can one fish, farm, or plow the soil?

Perhaps because of these difficulties, Mahavira's faith did not become as popular or as widespread as that of the Buddha. Still, the religion he founded—Jainism—remains important. There are more than 2 million Jainists in India and Pakistan today.

ALEXANDER THE GREAT ARRIVES

About 250 years after the founding of these two new faiths, Alexander the Great appeared on the middle reaches of the Indus River. It is often said that 326 B.C., the year of his appearance, is the first definite date in the history of the Indian subcontinent. Alexander crossed the Indus and fought a battle against King Porus of the Punjab. Porus had elephants, the first Alexander's troops had seen. The battle was fierce, but Alexander prevailed, as he usually did. He and Porus then became friends and firm allies.

Confident in his destiny, Alexander wanted to push on into India. His Macedonian soldiers, however, weary of a decade of military campaigns, staged a sit-down protest against their leader. They refused to go any farther. They wanted to return to their wives and families in Macedonia.

Although he was furious over his men's disobedience, Alexander agreed to return home. He built a fleet of boats, and the Macedonian Army floated down the length of the Indus River. Alexander divided his army into two sections. The first (and luckier) group of men boarded the boats and sailed along the Arabian coast on their way back to Persia. The second group went overland with Alexander, through the deserts of lower Baluchistan.

The Gedrosian Desert, through which Alexander and his men marched, is one of the most inhospitable places on Earth. Many men died from the harsh conditions. Alexander and the hardiest soldiers survived. They came out of the desert and reached Babylon, Mesopotamia, where Alexander died at the age of 31 or 32. During his short, whirlwind life, Alexander had impacted the lives of people from the Straits of Dardanelles in what is now Turkey to the banks of the Indus River.

THE MAURYAN KINGDOM

Pakistani tradition states that in his brief six months on the banks of the Indus, Alexander met an ambitious young Indian prince named Chandragupta. This man saw Alexander's power and grandeur and decided to emulate him. Within 30 years of Alexander's departure, Chandragupta had built the foundations of the first truly indigenous kingdom of the Indian subcontinent. Centered in what is now northwestern India and Pakistan, the new Mauryan kingdom extended for nearly 1,000 miles (1,609 kilometers) along an east-west line.

Chandragupta's grandson Ashoka (also spelled *Asoka*) became the most renowned of the Mauryan kings. More is known about Ashoka than any previous Indian leader because of the edicts his officials carved in stones. These edicts tell a story of an ambitious, warlike king, who converted to Buddhism and then came close to becoming a true "philosopher-king."

Ashoka made war on his neighbors, the Kringalis, in his youth, and was appalled by the death and destruction he caused. Changing his mind and his life, he became a Buddhist, and had edicts carved. Reminders of the sanctity of life, Ashoka's edicts are among the best-known depictions of a personal religious conversion from ancient history.

The Mauryan Dynasty weakened after Ashoka's death, and it was in ruins by the time of Jesus Christ's birth. In the centuries

Located near Taxila, in the Punjab region, Dharmarajika Stupa is the oldest Buddhist monument in Pakistan. One of eight shrines built during the reign (273 to 232 B.C.) of the Mauryan king Ashoka, the stupa was used to house relics of the Buddha.

that followed, Pakistan and northern India were overrun by countless invasions from the north, over the Khyber Pass route. In Western history, these invaders are known as the Scythians (horse people of the plains of southern Russia), but on the sub-continent they are known as the Sakas, a group that established a kingdom that lasted for nearly 200 years. They were followed by the Kushans and others.

In the sixth century A.D., a Chinese monk came to Pak-istan and India, looking for relics of the Buddha. Known as

Hsuan-tsang, this remarkable man made it from China to India over the Himalayas, and, after a stay of nearly 20 years, he returned the same way, taking with him hundreds of Buddhist books and relics. Chinese Buddhism is descended from this one man's efforts.

ISLAM

Shortly after Hsuan-tsang's trip to India, yet another religion was about to appear. It made itself known in the seventh century A.D., and found its way to the subcontinent in the eighth century. This was Islam, or the Muslim faith (Muslim means "one who submits to the will of Allah [the Muslim name for God]").

Founded by the Prophet Muhammad around 620 A.D., the new faith spread rapidly from its birthplace on the Arabian Peninsula. Fortified by this strict new monotheistic faith, the Arabs conquered Persia, took most of North Africa, and entered Spain in 711.

At about the same time, Arab Muslims first arrived in Pakistan. Unlike most invaders, they came by sea, landing near the mouth of the Indus River. Within one generation, the Arabs had become masters of the Sind. This group of conquerors did not expand farther. They remained in the Sind, giving that area a different character from the rest of Pakistan for some time.

Full-scale Muslim invasions came later, through the Khyber Pass. Muhammad of Ghazni, known to many Muslim scholars as a Defender of the Faith and to many outsiders as a bandit and plunderer, made no less than 17 invasions of Pakistan and northern India. Muhammad did not succeed in his goal of creating a Muslim Pakistan, but many of the tribal peoples in the northwest were converted to Islam during the eleventh and twelfth centuries.

THE DELHI SULTANATE

A true Muslim state was first set up around 1325, when the Delhi Sultanate was established. The sultans who ruled a swath of northern India and Pakistan did so loosely, giving much authority to regional rulers. It was a Muslim state, but it was not a theocracy. The period of the Delhi Sultanate (1325–1526) was marked by better relations between Hindus and Muslims than would later be the case.

In the last few decades of the Delhi Sultanate, two new holy men arose to suggest new ways of understanding. Guru Nanak and Kabir were contemporaries. Born in the city of Benares, Guru Nanak led a normal life until his thirties, when he experienced an awakening. Its basic message was quite simple: "There is no Hindu, there is no Mussalman [Muslim]" in the eyes of God. If ever there was a messenger and a message who had a hope to unite India's religions, it was Guru Nanak.

Born in northern India about the same time as Guru Nanak, Kabir was a free spirit who avoided nearly all formal religion. When asked what faith he followed, Kabir replied, "No book, no creed." Kabir disliked the caste system, formalized Hinduism, and the conflicts between Hindus and Muslims in India. Kabir is remembered today as a great saint, revered by Hindus and Muslims alike. Guru Nanak is known as the founder of the new faith of the Sikhs. Blending aspects of both Hinduism and Islam, the Sikhs came to dominate the land of the Punjab.

Guru Nanak was a peaceful man, but in the mid-seventeenth century, the Sikhs became known as warriors. They were hired as bodyguards, treasure keepers, and mercenaries. By the time the British came to India and Pakistan in the nineteenth century, the Sikhs were considered the best fighters on the subcontinent.

THE MUGHAL EMPIRE

All previous invasions or incursions into the region had come either through the northwestern passes or by a short sea trip from Persia. In the early sixteenth century, two new invasions came, including one by a very long route, completely around Africa.

These two invasions came at almost exactly the same moment. In 1526, Babur, who was a Turco-Mongol, invaded Pakistan through the Khyber Pass. He defeated the armies of the Delhi Sultanate and by the time of his death in 1530, he had set the early foundation of what would become the Mughal Empire (1526–1760). *Mughal* is a corruption of the word *Mongol*. Babur was a descendant of both Genghis Khan and Tamerlane, the great Mongol leaders. Just the same, Babur brought a tradition of interest in art, poetry, and flowers that gave his Mughal Dynasty a very different public image from that of the early Mongols. This interest in art and culture continued through Babur's descendants. His grandson Aurangzeb built Pakistan's second-largest mosque (Muslim house of worship), the Badshahi Masjid, while his great-grandson Shah Jehan built the Taj Mahal.

In about the same year that Babur arrived from the northwest, Portuguese sailors and missionaries arrived in the southern parts of the subcontinent. The Portuguese came to India searching for the spices of the East. They built forts along the southern coast of India to resupply their ships as their sailors went all the way to the Spice Islands of Indonesia.

The Mughal descendants of Babur ruled the northern region of India and Pakistan. They made their capital at Lahore, today the center of Pakistani cultural and intellectual life. Their summer capital, built to escape the tremendous heat of the Punjab, was located in Sringhar, Kashmir.

Meanwhile, the Portuguese continued to hold small sections of southern India. The Portuguese, however, were replaced by the Dutch in the seventeenth century, who were then supplanted by the British and the French in the eighteenth century.

THE BRITISH RAJ

In 1757, Englishman Robert Clive won an important battle at Plassey in eastern India. From that day on, it became clear that the British would dominate the southern part of the subcontinent.

Badshahi Masjid, or the King's Mosque, was completed in 1673 by the Mughal emperor Aurangzeb. Located in Lahore, the capital of the Punjab, the mosque is the second largest in Pakistan and can hold up to 60,000 worshippers.

Clive's success, however, was not immediately followed up by British officials. For the next 80 years, the British East India Company managed British interests in India as a private, commercial concern. Only after the "Great Mutiny" of 1857–1858 did the British government change its policy. Queen Victoria became Empress of India, and India (including Pakistan) became the "jewel in the crown" of the British Empire.

The British Raj (the word *raj* derives from "one who rules") was a mixture of benevolence and despotism. The British thoroughly controlled southern India, but left a number of northern sections in the hands of local rulers such as maharajas. Pakistan, the western frontier of British India, was treated with great importance. Not only was this area vulnerable to Russian invasion, but the British also saw other things of great value in Pakistan, particularly the people.

After two short but bloody wars, the British defeated the Sikhs in 1849 and annexed the Punjab. Meanwhile, the British went even farther north, into Afghanistan, but they were defeated by Afghan tribesmen during the First Anglo-Afghan War (1838–1842), which saw the virtual annihilation of a British force outside Kabul. From then on, the British sought to control the passes, rather than attempt to pacify the people of the mountains. The Pashtuns have never been truly subjugated by anyone.

Between about 1860 and 1920, the British brought significant improvements to India and Pakistan. Irrigation projects in the Punjab were begun through British initiative. The city of Karachi's value was recognized, and its population began to grow under British rule. Perhaps even more important, the Sikhs, Muslims, Hindus, Christians, Zoroastrians, and others of the subcontinent knew they had equal status under British law, as long as they were not accused of assaulting or robbing a *Sahib*, or white-skinned ruler.

THE PARTITION OF INDIA

After about 1920, however, enthusiasm for the British government waned. The Muslim League, founded in 1906, began to develop the idea of an independent Muslim Republic in Pakistan. Meanwhile, Mohandas Gandhi and others carried out a program of nonviolent resistance to British rule.

The British officers and viceroy simply considered Gandhi a nuisance at first. During the 1930s, though, as he conducted hunger strikes and continued to insist on practicing nonviolent forms of protest, the British began to see the power of this movement. World War II drained the British treasury and the will of the British people to maintain their great overseas empire. By early 1947, negotiations for a British withdrawal from the subcontinent were becoming paramount.

From the beginning, Gandhi had dreamed, written, and spoken of a united India—a single India that could not be divided by religion, ethnicity, or other conditions. In the months that preceded independence, Muhammad Ali Jinnah, leader of the Muslim League, began to demand that two— rather than one—nations be created after the British evacuated, one for Hindus and one for Muslims. Gandhi resisted bitterly, claiming that, "The right eye of India is Hindu, and its left eye is Muslim." It was Jinnah's vision that prevailed, however, and at midnight on August 15, 1947, two countries were officially created from the region that had been the British Raj (Pakistan held its official ceremony a day earlier).

American readers who opened the *New York Times* found articles about the Indian subcontinent all through the opening page and sections:

INDIA AND PAKISTAN BECOME NATIONS;
CLASHES CONTINUE
Ceremonies at New Delhi and Karachi Mark
Independence for 400,000,000 Persons.
New Delhi, Friday, Aug. 15—India achieved her long-sought independence today through the transfer of British power to two dominions into which that land of 400,000,000 persons has been divided: India and Pakistan.

Ceremonies in New Delhi proclaimed the new nation of India. Ceremonies in Karachi commemorated the birth of the new nation of Pakistan. The Indian subcontinent, indeed the Asian world, would never be the same again.

5

People and Culture

Since British author Rudyard Kipling's spy novel *Kim* was published in 1901, millions of readers around the world have been entertained by the story of the adolescent boy, the old Tibetan lama (monk), and the middle-aged horse trader. *Kim* is a magnificent coming-of-age tale that combines remarkable storytelling with messages about the peoples and religions of British India. At one point in the book, the orphan boy Kim, who had an English father and an Indian mother, asks the horse trader Mahbub Ali:

"What am I? Mussalman, Hindu, Jain, or Buddhist? That is a hard knot." Mahbub Ali replied:

Thou art beyond question an unbeliever, and therefore thou wilt be damned. So says my Law—or I think it does. But thou art also my Little Friend of all the World, and I love thee. So says my heart. This matter of creeds is like horseflesh. The wise man knows horses are good—that there is profit to be made from all; and for myself—but that I am a good Sunni and hate the men of Tirah—I could believe the same of all the Faiths. Now manifestly a Kathiawar mare taken from the sands of her birthplace and removed to the west of Bengal founders—nor is even a Balkh stallion (and there are no better horses than those of Balkh, were they not so heavy in the shoulder) of any account in the great Northern deserts beside the snow-camels I have seen. Therefore I say in my heart the Faiths are like the horses. Each has merit in its own country.

Though they were written in 1901, these words aptly describe the questions that continue to plague the people of Pakistan. Although 97 percent of them today are Muslim, they are descendants of Hindus, Persians, Jews, Zoroastrians, and others.

About 166 million people (2006 estimate) live in Pakistan. The nation's peoples are just as diverse as the landscape they inhabit. The Pakistanis display a great mixture of physical and cultural types, a mixture created by the numerous migrations and invasions that have occurred over the centuries. Roughly speaking, the major groups are Punjabis, Sindhis, Pashtuns, Mohajirs, Baluchis, Brahuis, Kalashas, Burushos, Wahis, Baltis, Gujars, and refugees from Afghanistan. It is important to remember that this melting pot of peoples has existed for hundreds, if not thousands of years, even though the state of Pakistan is only slightly more than 50 years old.

PUNJABIS

The Punjabis are Pakistan's majority population. Based in the land of the Punjab, they are a distinct and recognizable group. Punjabis tend to be taller than many of their fellow Pakistanis, and they generally have lighter skin than most of the peoples to the south. It is likely that the Punjabis are of Aryan descent, but

Wagah is the ceremonial border between northwestern India and northeastern Pakistan, in the Punjab region. Each evening, Pakistani and Indian soldiers lower their country's flag, shake hands, and then close the gate that separates the two nations.

their point of origin is as mysterious to them as it is to outsiders. They share a long heritage of life in the Punjab and a well-earned reputation as fierce warriors. When the British first entered the Punjab in the 1840s, they designated the Punjabis a warrior people, and recruited many of them to serve in Queen Victoria's army.

The Punjabis have also endured a severe and painful split. The partition in 1947 left 63 percent of the Punjab in Pakistan's hands and the rest in India. Millions of people on both sides of the border feel the pain of the partition to this day. The bus ride from Amritsar, India, to Lahore, Pakistan, is the only point of entry that can connect long-separated families. Only in the Punjab, on both sides of the border, is there a strong sentiment for ending the partition and making the two countries one. In other parts of Pakistan, the idea of a reunion with India is considered impossible and undesirable.

A large majority of the administrators and leaders of the modern nation of Pakistan have been Punjabis. This numerical dominance is often resented by other Pakistani peoples, but the physical position of the Punjab—its centrality to the country—has made it almost an established fact that Punjabis will have the most influence in governmental affairs.

SINDHIS

Sindhis live in the province of Sind, on the eastern side of the lower Indus River. Sindhis have long been perceived as a people living apart from the rest of Pakistan. This is because the desert areas of the Sind have isolated them from the north, and because this is where the Muslim faith first came to Pakistan in A.D. 711. Sindhis tend to see themselves as the "original" Muslims of Pakistan, and they view all the others as newcomers to the faith. Sindhis feel underrepresented at the high levels of government. They resent the fact that the Sind city of Karachi—which was once the country's capital—is often seen as a political back-water, and that nearly all decisions are made to the north in Islamabad. Within the great city of Karachi, many Sindhis resent the presence of the Mohajirs (refugees).

Physically, it is not easy to identify the Sindhis. They may be darker in complexion than the Punjabis, but enough cross-mixtures have occurred that the Sindhis tend to identify themselves culturally rather than physically.

One of the most extensive studies of the Sindhis was done in the mid-nineteenth century by British traveler and explorer Richard F. Burton. While studying the burial practices of the Sindhis, Burton commented:

> Every traveler in Sind must have remarked the immense tracts of graveyards which it contains. The reason of this disproportion between the cities of the dead and those of the living is, in the first place, that the people are fond of burying their kin in spots which are celebrated for sanctity, and secondly, they believe that by interring corpses close to the dust of their forefathers, the Ruham or souls of the departed, will meet and commune together after death. Hence it is that when a Sindhi dies in a foreign place, his heirs or friends will generally agree to remove the body to the family graveyard, at a certain period or within a stated time. The corpse is then exhumed, and carried in a box on horse or camel-back to its final destination. And it is believed that when such promise has been given, the two angels never visit the provisional tomb, but defer their questioning till the second interment takes place.

THE PASHTUNS

The easiest Pakistani cultural group to identify is the Pashtun, who live in the Northwest Frontier Province and are cut off by the Afghan border from their relatives in Afghanistan. The Pashtuns are tall, slender, dark-haired, and are often characterized by their language. They are very proud that they were never assimilated by the numerous conquerors who came through their region.

The Pashtuns, who are the world's largest autonomous tribal group, have a deep and powerful social code that governs nearly all their actions. Known as *Pashtunwali* ("Way of the Pashtun"), the code is extremely male-centered. Pashtun men are expected to be cheerful, brave, and always hospitable. If a Pashtun accepts a stranger into his home—however briefly—the Pashtun is expected to put all the needs and desires of his visitor above his own and to be completely at the service of his guest. This part of the code, called *Melmastia,* can extend to dangerous situations. If, for example, a guest is a criminal or a wanted person, the host is expected to lay down his own life if necessary to protect the guest. Very few exceptions are allowed to this rule.

Badal is the second part of the Pashtun code. *Badal* means "revenge," and Pashtun men are duty bound to seek revenge for offenses, hostilities, and even for minor slights on their honor. Pashtuns are expected to wreak havoc either on the person who committed the offense, or on that person's family. There is no statute of limitations: Vengeance is often taken many years after the offense was committed. This part of the code has led to endless feuds and counterfeuds, which have caused the Pashtuns to lose the strength to resist outside forces.

Nanwatai is the third aspect of the code. It means "formal abasement." Because Pashtuns often fight each other, *Nanwatai* is meant to preserve the lives of the losers. The defeated are expected to show absolute submission to the victors, who are expected to be merciful and generous.

Nang, which means "honor," is the fourth part of the code. It refers to the duty of a Pashtun man to defend the honor of the women of his family or clan. Sometimes, *Nang* is taken to such an extreme that a Pashtun will seek retribution if an outsider takes a long look at a woman. This part of the code makes it very difficult for outsiders to infiltrate Pashtun clans.

Relations between the federal government in Islamabad and the Pashtuns are tricky at best. Pakistan recognizes the Pashtuns as an autonomous tribal group, and they do not pay taxes or vote in elections. Even so, they are recognized as one of the most important ethnic groups within Pakistan—and certainly the most dangerous.

THE BALUCHIS

The second-largest tribal group in Pakistan is the Baluchi, who live in the arid areas of Baluchistan, in southwest and central-west Pakistan. The Baluchis are probably of Turco-Iranian descent, and they have good relations with their relatives on the Iranian side of the border. For centuries, the Baluchis have managed to live in semi-independence, because the region they inhabit is one of the most barren landscapes on Earth. There are occasional oases, but Baluchistan stretches for hundreds of miles across salty deserts that intimidate most travelers. Images taken from space show that Baluchistan suffers from numerous sandstorms created by winds that come from the Arabian Sea and kick up dust overland. Only the hardiest people can live here, and the Baluchis are legendary for their endurance, good humor, and hospitality. A poem from Muhammad Iqbal, "An Old Baluchi to his Son," shows the love of the Baluchis for their landscape:

> Winds of these wastelands be your love! Bokhara,
> Delhi, are worth no more. Like running water
> Go where they will: these desert plains are ours, and
> Ours are these valleys.

Few Westerners spend any time in Baluchistan, but those who have report a Baluchi ritual called *hal*. When two Baluchis meet after a length of time, they are required to tell each other everything that has happened since their last meeting. The ritual is taken quite seriously, and sometimes the conversation lasts for hours. Nothing is allowed to be passed over. The few foreigners who wish to marry into the Baluchi tribe often bemoan the number of intimate details they must relate to their new countrymen.

The Baluchi tribe, who live in the southwestern and central-western Pakistan province of Baluchistan, are expert horsemen and herders. Every February, thousands of Baluchi tribesmen gather in the town of Sibi to participate in a mela, or festival, which includes the horse dance (pictured here).

The Baluchis are first-rate horsemen and nomadic herders. They move their flocks from south to north during the summer months, and then reverse the process during the winter.

THE MOHAJIRS

A group that is identified by status rather than tribe is the *Mohajir*, which means "refugee." At the time of the partition in 1947, hundreds of thousands of immigrants crossed the border from India to Pakistan. Most of them settled in Sind, where they are known as Mohajirs. Many of them received upper-class educations and had professional skills, and as a result, the Mohajirs have displaced many native Sindhis from positions of prominence. This has led to a degree of enmity against the Mohajirs. The last few decades have witnessed occasional out-breaks of violence against the newcomers. Tension is highest in Karachi, where the Mohajirs make up perhaps two-thirds of the city's population.

OTHER ETHNIC GROUPS

After the Punjabi, Sindhi, Pashtun, and Mohajir, there are a number of much smaller ethnic groups in Pakistan. One is the Brahui of central Baluchistan. Differences between Brahuis and Baluchis are not immediately apparent to an outsider, but the two peoples do not mix. The Brahuis claim to be direct descendants of the Prophet Muhammad. Linguistically and physically, however, they appear instead to be descendants of the original inhabitants of the Indus River valley, prior to the Aryan invasions.

Another small group is the Kalasha, also known as the Kafirs (nonbelievers), and sometimes as the Nuri. The Kalashas live in a handful of mountain villages on the border between Afghanistan and Pakistan, in the extreme northern part of the Northwest Frontier Province. The Kalashas are apparently not related to the Pashtuns, or to any other ethnic groups in the area. Until about 1900, the Kalashas were most distinctive for being non-Muslims in an area that was heavily Islamic in its composi-tion. Many Kalashas were forced to convert by the emir (leader) of Afghanistan after the turn of the twentieth century, but the converted and nonconverted members of the tribe seem to live peacefully together. Their principal town is Kamdesh.

Not all tribal groups have the full rights of citizens, and not all of them want those rights. Northern tribal peoples live in semiautonomous areas that are not part of the commonwealth.

They are administered by an agency that reports directly to the federal government in Islamabad.

Pakistan contains a great variety of peoples. This is largely because of the many invasions and conquests that have occurred over the centuries, but trade also has played an important part. From the time of Mohenjo-daro and Harappa, people have moved up and down the Indus River, across the Punjab, through the Khyber Pass, and into Afghanistan. The northern mountain areas have been more secluded, less influenced by passing conquerors and merchants. Even there, however, different villages and clans sometimes display an astounding variety of customs and attitudes.

Given the great diversity that exists among the peoples of Pakistan, it makes sense to follow the sentiments of the horse-trader in the novel *Kim*, that the faiths and peoples are like horses: They all have merit in their own region.

CHAPTER

6

The Islamic Republic of Pakistan

S aladin was a twelfth-century Kurdish general who led Muslim armies against the Christian European crusaders. He recaptured the city of Jerusalem in 1187, and allowed the Christians there to be ransomed by their relatives in Europe. This humane approach to conquest differed greatly from the brutal massacre carried out by the crusaders when they captured the city in 1099. For this and other reasons, Saladin remains one of the great heroes of Islam. As renowned author and anthropologist Akbar S. Ahmed wrote in his 1997 book, *Jinnah, Pakistan and Islamic Identity: The Search for Saladin*, "Among Muslims, Saladin's name is synonymous with courage, compassion, integrity and respect for culture." It is natural that Pakistanis—and other Muslims around the world—would look for his modern-day equivalent.

Pakistan became a nation on August 14, 1947. It is one of a handful of states that were born in the immediate aftermath of World War

II: India, Israel, and East and West Germany are other members of that group. Pakistan may be a very new country, but its roots are deep in the cross currents of South Asia and the Middle East.

MUHAMMAD ALI JINNAH

Young nations naturally search for heroes. England looks to King Alfred; Russia looks to Peter the Great; and the United States had a ready-made first leader in George Washington. Pakistan likewise had a hero ready the day it became a nation. His name was Muhammad Ali Jinnah.

Jinnah was born in Karachi in 1876. His parents were comfortable, middle-class Muslims, and he grew up in an environment that recalled the earlier, glorious days of Muslim unity. The late nineteenth century was not a good time for Muslims around the world. They saw their once-great countries and empires fall into the hands of foreigners (mostly the British), and the Arab Muslim world had fallen far behind the West, particularly in the area of military technology. Jinnah was one of a number of twentieth-century Muslim leaders who would work hard to reverse this trend. He would meet with considerable, though long-delayed success.

Jinnah went to London as a young man and studied law at Lincoln's Inn. He became a barrister (lawyer) by the age of 20, and when he returned to Karachi, he was practically the only Muslim attorney in what is now Pakistan. Handsome, impeccably dressed, and often haughty with strangers, Jinnah became a familiar face to the British government and to fellow Muslim leaders on the subcontinent.

Like most people, Jinnah was not as one-sided as he often appeared. Although he spent his life working for a country that would separate Muslims from Hindus, Jinnah married a Parsee (Zoroastrian). This aspect of his life is virtually off-limits for anyone conversing with a Pakistani today. Pakistanis remain mystified that their greatest leader could have married outside their faith.

Muhammad Ali Jinnah (left), pictured here with Mohandas Gandhi in September 1944, was largely responsible for helping Pakistan achieve independence. Today, Jinnah is revered as a great leader in Pakistan and both the dates of his birth and death are national holidays.

Jinnah's relations with Mohandas "Mahatma" Gandhi remain somewhat mysterious. Several photographs seem to show that the two men liked and trusted each other, but there are also indications that each distrusted the power and influence of the other. The two leaders could not have been more different. Jinnah was elegant and urbane; Gandhi was purposely "dressed down" and identified with the poorer elements of Indian society. Despite their personal differences, Jinnah and Gandhi were two of the four men who determined the future of the subcontinent at the time of partition. The other two were Jawaharlal Nehru and Lord Louis Mountbatten, the last British viceroy (governor).

By early 1947, Jinnah was at odds with the other three men. Gandhi and Nehru wanted a united India—one flag for the entire subcontinent. Jinnah believed that he and his fellow Muslims would be oppressed by Hindu rule. Desperate to keep the subcontinent together, Gandhi and Mountbatten offered Jinnah a handsome bribe: to be the first prime minister of a united India. Jinnah refused. His stubbornness led to the partition of the subcontinent between India and Pakistan in August 1947.

Few people at that time knew that Jinnah was dying. He was suffering from tuberculosis and the strain of two decades as the leader of the Muslim movement. Despite his arrogant demeanor, Jinnah was a sensitive man who suffered from the criticism he received. He died on September 11, 1948, just one year after his dream of a Pakistani nation had come to fruition.

Jinnah's death made him an instant hero to the Pakistanis. Even today, he has no rival. He was and is the *Quaid-i-Azam* ("Great Leader"). Many people throughout the Middle East consider Jinnah one of the great Muslim leaders of all time. Some equate him with Saladin, the warrior-king who fought against the crusaders and who won Jerusalem for the Muslims.

PAKISTAN AFTER THE PARTITION

With Jinnah's passing, Pakistan settled into a more secure but less joyful time. There were numerous pressing problems. First was Pakistan's relationship with India. Second was the division between East Pakistan, centered on the Ganges River and the Bay of Bengal, and West Pakistan, centered on the Indus River and the Arabian Sea. The two problems fed into each other, because 1,000 miles (1,600 kilometers) of Indian soil lay between East and West Pakistan. Almost from the start, there were critics who claimed Pakistan was based on a flawed concept and could not endure.

The 1950s nearly proved the critics right. Tensions continued between Pakistan and India, and East and West Pakistan had serious strains in their relationship. Since the only strongly uniting factor was religion, Pakistan changed its name and approach to government in 1956. Its new title was the Islamic Republic of Pakistan.

To the credit of the government, there was no organized system against minorities in Pakistan. The official policy was toleration, but even so, minority communities stayed the same or shrank in size as the Muslim population increased by leaps and bounds. When Pakistan was formed in 1947, Muslims made up about 80 percent of the population; by 2000, they comprised 97 percent of the total.

No leader of Jinnah's stature emerged during the 1950s. Pakistan seemed to be stagnant in many ways. Meanwhile, India became more powerful, both in terms of population and in military strength, and Pakistan became concerned about its dangerous neighbor.

The 1960s were, on the whole, positive for Pakistan. Relations with India improved modestly, and Pakistan made important moves forward in irrigation, building the Tarbela Dam and bringing electricity to many parts of the country. Military leader General Ayub Khan inspired a good deal of confidence.

If there was one burning issue that was often swept under the rug, it was population growth. Pakistan's population increased from about 70 million to 100 million people between 1950 and 1980, and the explosion was particularly felt in urban areas. Karachi, which had been a quiet city of half a million people in 1945, suddenly became an urban jungle with nearly 10 million residents in 1980, and perhaps as many as 14 million by the year 2000. As quickly as Pakistan worked to irrigate the deserts and increase food production, the population bomb continued to tick, louder and louder.

Then came the beginning of the 1970s, and almost immediately, Pakistan was thrown into crisis. The divided state, located at the two wings of the subcontinent, was torn in two, and India took advantage of the situation to defeat the Pakistani army.

THE 1971 WAR AND BANGLADESH

Tensions had existed between East and West Pakistan for some time. The two sections were about as different as could be. Hot, tropical, and densely populated East Pakistan resented the level of governmental control that came first from Karachi and then from Islamabad, and that its economy had been exploited by West Pakistan for years. West Pakistan, half desert and half irrigated land, could not identify with its eastern counterpart, which seemed too far away and different. Then came the tragedy of 1971.

It was a time of conflict around the globe. The Vietnam War was still going on, although the United States was withdrawing its troops. The Arab-Israeli conflict was simmering, and would break into yet another war in October 1973. The "time of troubles" had begun in Northern Ireland about two years before. The cold war between the capitalist United States and Communist Soviet Union was ongoing. Now, added to all this, came a war between Pakistan and India.

The 1971 war lay to rest the idea that the Muslims of Pakistan were natural soldiers and the Hindus of India were natural cowards. India won most of the battles, and took about 100,000 Pakistanis prisoner. These prisoners of war languished in Indian jails for some time. Even worse, though, was the loss of East Pakistan. In the midst of the war with India, East Pakistan announced that it intended to be its own sovereign nation, separate from West Pakistan. Although there were attempts to change this course, both by force and by negotiation, the die was cast. In the autumn of 1971, what had been East Pakistan became the new nation of Bangladesh.

It was a grim time for Pakistanis. They hunkered down and determined to wait for the situation to get better. To a large extent, the next 20 years brought only more of the same: poverty, illiteracy, rapid population growth, and continued tensions with neighboring countries.

In the wake of the loss of East Pakistan, the now smaller country wrote a new constitution. The Constitution of 1973 provides for a chief of state (president), a head of the government (prime minister), and a bicameral legislature (parliament). Even more than earlier documents, the 1973 Constitution states that Pakistan is a Muslim nation and that Islam is the recognized faith of the Pakistani people.

The new constitution did not keep Pakistanis from what one author has called "the search for Saladin." As a young, insecure nation, Pakistan naturally gravitated to charismatic leaders who promised dramatic solutions to national problems. One such leader was Zulfikar Ali Bhutto; another was his charismatic daughter Benazir Bhutto.

LEADERSHIP OF THE BHUTTOS

Lineage is important in Pakistan, and the Bhutto clan has been important in Sindhi politics for generations. They claim descent from the earliest Muslim invaders in the eighth century A.D. Zulfikar founded the Pakistan Peoples Party in 1967 and became prime minister of Pakistan in 1974. He was slowly edged out by the military leader General Muhammad Zia-ul-Haq. Bhutto was put in prison in 1977, and executed in May 1979. In her autobiography, Benazir Bhutto recalled the event:

> I stood in a daze, not believing what had happened to my father, not wanting to. It was just not possible that Zulfikar Ali Bhutto, the first prime minister of Pakistan

to be elected directly by the people, was dead. Where there had been repression under the generals who had ruled Pakistan since its birth in 1947, my father had been the first to bring democracy. Where the people had lived as they had for centuries at the mercy of their tribal chiefs and landlords, he had installed Pakistan's first Constitution to guarantee legal protection and civil rights.

General Zia proceeded to establish a full-scale military dictatorship. He is remembered fondly by many Pakistanis today, not for his methods, but because he was a pious Muslim who attempted to bring the country more fully into compliance with the dictates of Islam.

Because of economic aid from the United States, which was spurred by the Soviet invasion of neighboring Afghanistan, Pakistan enjoyed relative political stability in the mid-1980s.

Pakistanis were looking forward to better times when Benazir Bhutto flew from London, England, to Lahore in 1986. She was welcomed by more than one million people, but it is difficult to say whether this outpouring of support was also a condemnation of Zia's government. Benazir Bhutto ran her own election campaign for prime minister in 1988. It did not look promising; General Zia managed to have many of her supporters banned from the polls in advance. On August 17, 1988, however, Zia's plane crashed, and the general was killed. All of Pakistan looked to Benazir Bhutto, and on December 1, 1988, she became prime minister, and the first woman ever to lead a Muslim nation.

Although she promised to make several social reforms, including repealing a number of controversial laws that restricted women's rights, Benazir Bhutto never lived up to her image as a tireless and faithful public servant. During her two terms as prime minister (1988–1991 and 1993–1996), corruption increased within Pakistan's government. Bhutto also proved as unable to make any headway on the issue of Kashmir

Benazir Bhutto, pictured here at a ceremony celebrating the forty-eighth anniversary of Pakistan's independence in 1995, served two terms as prime minister of Pakistan. In 1996, Bhutto's government was dismissed due to charges of corruption, and she currently resides in Dubai, United Arab Emirates.

as any of the men who had preceded her in office. In 2002, President Pervez Musharaff introduced a new amendment to Pakistan's constitution that restricts prime ministers from running for reelection after serving two terms. This disqualifies Bhutto from returning to office; however, she continues to support the Pakistan Peoples Party from here home in Dubai, United Arab Emirates, where she has lived since 2004.

NUCLEAR TESTS AND INTERNATIONAL RELATIONS

Bhutto alternated as prime minister with Nawaz Sharif, who served from 1990 to 1993, and then from 1997 to 1999. Under his leadership, Pakistan achieved a long-desired goal: the production of nuclear weapons. Coming at the same time as the announcement of India's nuclear success, the news had a sobering effect on leaders around the world.

Early in May 1998, India conducted seven nuclear tests, all of them in the Thar Desert, which borders Pakistan. Just two weeks later, Pakistan responded with five successful nuclear tests of its own. Suddenly, there was no mistaking the fact that the subcontinent now had two major powers, both of which had nuclear capability.

Both Indians and Pakistanis responded with great enthusiasm to the tests. There was—as one commentator put it—little else for either nation to cheer about. If this was true of India, it was even truer of Pakistan, because the 1990s had seen a gradual erosion of the economy and the faith of the Pakistani people in their government.

Pakistan had been propped up by economic and military support from the United States during the 1980s. As long as Soviet tanks and soldiers were stationed in neighboring Afghanistan, the United States increased its aid to Pakistan each year, and the economy enjoyed moderate prosperity. Even supporters of General Zia acknowledged that he did not use this brief time of prosperity to remedy the social ills of Pakistan. Instead, the money was funneled to the military, and specifically, to the nuclear weapons program.

U.S. economic aid dwindled after the Soviets left Afghanistan in 1989, and even more so after the collapse of the

Soviet Union in 1991. Pakistani-U.S. relations deteriorated even further after the nuclear tests of 1998. American diplomats blamed both India and Pakistan for the rise in tensions on the subcontinent, and withheld economic aid from both nations.

Given all the bad news they had received during the decade, Pakistanis were not surprised when a military coup took place in October 1999. General Pervez Musharraf, the army chief of staff, led the coup when he learned that he was about to be dismissed by the prime minister. Musharraf took power in a three-hour coup, then relayed the news to the Pakistani people on television. Musharraf emphasized that he did not relish his new position, and he eventually gave up some of his powers to parliament in November 2002. In the meantime, however, he said he would attempt to deal with Pakistan's many social and economic ills. Then came the startling and tragic events of September 11, 2001.

TERRORISM AND MUSLIM EXTREMISTS

On September 11, 2001, Muslim extremists, many of them from Saudi Arabia and Egypt, hijacked four airplanes and crashed two of them into the World Trade Center in New York City. Another hit the Pentagon in Washington, D.C., and the fourth came down in the Pennsylvania countryside. Thousands of American civilians were killed and wounded, and the U.S. economy received a sharp jolt.

U.S. President George W. Bush proposed a tough new international campaign against terrorists. In his first major speech on the issue, Bush emphasized that the United States would not discriminate between terrorists and the regimes or countries that aided them. This put Pakistan on the spot. There was no question of Pakistan supporting terrorism, but Pakistan was one of only three countries that recognized the Taliban regime in Afghanistan that harbored the September 11 terrorists. Within hours of Bush's speech, President Musharraf faced a dilemma: Would he cooperate with the United States, or try to remain neutral in the coming conflict?

Musharraf decided to support the United States and in January 2002, he made a landmark speech in which he denounced Islamic extremism. He announced that Pakistan would allow U.S. planes the right to fly over Pakistan, and he broke off diplomatic relations with the Taliban regime. As the United States began bombing Taliban strongholds, Musharraf stayed loyal to his American ally, despite increasing pressure from Islamic groups at home.

By the beginning of 2002, it appeared that Musharraf's gamble had paid some dividends. Economic aid from the United States flowed to Pakistan once more, and the country was hailed for its role in the international war against terror. At almost exactly the same time, however, tensions between India and Pakistan threatened to undo all that Musharraf had accomplished.

PROBLEMS WITH INDIA

In the global climate that followed the September 11 attacks, India used the heightened anger over terrorism to focus attention on Pakistani groups in Kashmir. The Bush administration appeared more sympathetic to India than to Pakistan. As a result, Musharraf promised to round up and contain fundamentalist and terrorist groups inside Pakistan.

The support by the United States was a victory for India and a humiliation for Musharraf. Despite the United States's apparent favoritism toward India, Musharraf initiated talks with India in mid-2004 to address the dispute over Kashmir. Although little came out of the discussions, further dialogue is needed because the region remains a flashpoint between the two countries as they continue to build up their nuclear arsenals to defend their interests. Musharraf, however, has been praised by foreign observers for his moderation and steady purpose. If anyone could keep a lid on the very different elements within Pakistan, it seems to be Musharraf. In his moderation and willingness to compromise, Musharraf has shown some aspects of the type of leadership Muslims admire most: the leadership style of Saladin.

CHAPTER

7

Pakistan's Economy

In his 2000 book, *Taliban: Militant Islam, Oil and Fundamentalism in Central Asia*, Pakistani journalist Ahmed Rashid recounted why his country's economy had fallen on hard times: "In the 1980s the fall-out from the Soviet invasion of Afghanistan had created the 'heroin and kalashnikov culture' that undermined Pakistan's politics and economy." Pakistan is an upper-tier Third World country that aspires to join the ranks of the countries that boast developed economies. In the years since independence and partition, Pakistan has made numerous forward strides, but they have all been at least equaled by the rise in population and demand for food. To make matters worse, in the 1990s, Pakistan developed a black market, or underground economy, that amounted to more than one-third of the nation's total wealth. Opium production and heroin consumption threaten to undo much of the good that was achieved in the 1960s and 1980s.

AGRICULTURE AND POPULATION GROWTH

Like all countries, Pakistan's economy can be broken down into three major components: agriculture, industry, and trade. When independence was achieved in 1947, Pakistan was primarily an agricultural nation. Perhaps 80 percent of all Pakistanis were involved in the production or transportation of food. Today, that figure has dropped to between 50 and 55 percent, but there is little doubt that farming is still the backbone of Pakistani life. Without it, the nation would quickly become destitute.

The so-called Green Revolution came to Pakistan in the mid-1960s. American and European scientists extracted the fastest-growing seeds for wheat and rice and exported them to many countries of the Third World. Rice production soared in parts of Southeast Asia, and East Pakistan, which is now Bangladesh, was a recipient of that increase.

West Pakistan benefited both from the new cotton and wheat seed types, and from the importation of new farm machinery. Pakistan's food crops increased significantly during the 1960s and early 1970s. However, its overall population increased as well.

Pakistan faces one of the multifaceted problems encountered by most Third World countries: that of trying to balance increased food production, better health care, and a soaring population. The first two factors are definite positives, in that people live healthier and longer lives. If the rate of births does not begin to decrease, though, Pakistan will head toward a population increase dangerously close to levels at which there will not be enough food for the people to eat. This has also been the case in India, Bangladesh, and many other Third World countries. Even Communist China, which rigorously controls its population growth, has expanded to become the largest society in human history.

THE ISSUE OF IRRIGATION

Wheat is the primary crop farmed throughout Pakistan. Irrigation projects along the Indus River and its tributaries have

Wheat is the primary agricultural product of Pakistan and many fields, such as these in northern Pakistan, are watered by the Indus River. Much of the northern stretches of the Indus and its tributaries have been dammed to provide irrigation to these crops; as a result, much of southern Pakistan has become barren.

allowed for a sizable increase in the amount of arable land. Pakistanis now often farm in areas that their great-great-grandparents considered desert. This is a major improvement made through the system of irrigation set up by the British in the mid-nineteenth century, and continued by the modern nation of Pakistan. Irrigation, however, does have its critics and its flaws.

One of the major concerns is oversalinization of the land. When the land becomes overly saline (too salty), it slowly becomes useless. This might seem unlikely in Pakistan, where there is so much sand and desert, but there is a water table below the sand surface, and that water table has risen in recent years, clogging the arteries of some farming land. Second, there is the problem of farmers being dislocated when major construction projects, dams in particular, have such importance.

The Indus River and its five major tributaries have been dammed as much as possible. The result is that south of the Tarbela Dam, and especially in the province of Sind, the Indus no longer resembles the great river it was in previous days. Like the Colorado River between Arizona and California and the Columbia River in Washington and Oregon, the lower areas of the Indus flow with much-reduced volume and force.

The construction of these dams is generally viewed in a positive light. The dams allow for irrigation, which expands the amount of land that can be cultivated. But—and it is an enormous "but"—Tarbela Dam, which harnesses some of the force of the Indus River, is itself an impressive structure. It stands 469 feet (143 meters) high and is 8,997 feet (2,742 meters) wide.

Pakistan faces the severe dangers of salinity in the soil and drought, because its rivers no longer nourish the soil in the lower regions. If the level of salinity ever expanded to the point where much of the land in the Punjab became unfit for cultivation, Pakistan would be at the edge of complete famine and social collapse. A comment on the changing ideas about dams was offered by Indian scientist and activist Anuradgha Mittal:

> I was taught in school that India had become independent through a long struggle, and that if we wanted to maintain our independence, the country had to move forward with development: building dams, investing in high technology. I remember how, before movies, we'd

see a newsreel about the prime minister christening a new dam, after which they'd play the national anthem. I would get tears in my eyes.

Though she writes about India, Mittal could just as well be talking about Pakistan or any other Third World country. Later, Mittal came to a different conclusion about dams and their effect on Indian society:

The dams were actually death centers that displaced millions from their lands with no restitution, and those in power didn't care about the thousands of people they dispossessed or killed. I suddenly realized that human beings have a great capacity for making decisions that intentionally starve others. I wanted to know why.

Whether one agrees with Mittal or not, most scientists and developers today recognize the dangers of building dams that change river flow and alter the lives of many people. Imagine if the United States did not have the Great Lakes and did not border the Atlantic and Pacific oceans. Imagine that 90 percent of the nation's water came from the Ohio, Mississippi, and Missouri rivers. Think of the consequences if those waters were to be dammed upstream, creating large reservoirs. It might help the growth of cities and industries, but millions of American farmers would have to either move or change their way of life. That is exactly what millions of Indians and Pakistanis have gone through for the past two generations.

Today, Pakistan holds its own in the agricultural sphere. The country is self-sufficient in the staple crops of wheat, millet, and rice, and it even exports some wheat to other nations. However, Pakistan is built on an ecosystem that is stretched to its limit, and the continually increasing population may strain it even further in coming years.

Carpet-weaving is among those light industries in Pakistan that traditionally used child labor to produce goods. In recent years, there has been an international push to close sweatshops, which often employ children who are forced to work long hours for little pay. Pictured here is a young carpet weaver in Muridke, Pakistan (near Lahore), practicing his trade.

INDUSTRY

Industry is the second cornerstone of economic development. Pakistan's industrial sector was woefully backward when the country won independence in 1947. Just about the only industrial area in which the country was self-sufficient in that year was in the making of concrete, which has continued to be a moneymaker. British firms began making concrete in northern Pakistan in the 1920s, and the practice spread to the southern regions by the 1940s. Concrete remains one of the most important large-scale industries for the country.

Light industries have shown a much greater increase than heavy ones such as concrete throughout the 50 years since independence. Pakistanis have begun to make clothing in numerous small shops, many of which are labeled *sweatshops* by observers in developed industrial nations. Many of the clothes worn by Americans, Europeans, and Japanese are made in Pakistan.

Though it does not contribute to the balance of trade, gun making must be included among the major handicrafts and industries of Pakistan. One town—60 miles south of Peshawar—solely produces guns. The gun makers there claim they can replicate any gun from anywhere in the world within one week of seeing the original. It is a Wild West-type town in which people who have made recent purchases empty rounds of ammunition into the air. This rowdy influence is deplored by many upper-class Pakistanis, especially in the south. They complain that "Kalashnikov culture" has been brought by the exiles from Afghanistan. There may be some truth in this, but guns have been a staple of the Pakistani economy and of the life of its tribal peoples since the first firearms appeared in the eighteenth century.

Firearms are more dramatic than poppy flowers, but the latter are at least as important to the black market in Pakistan. There are many types of poppy flowers around the world, most of which are not capable of producing an altered state in human beings. But *Papaversomniferum*, which is grown in Pakistan and neighboring Afghanistan, is the substance that heroin and opium are made from.

OPIUM AND THE BLACK MARKET

Poppy fields abound in the Northwest Province and in the northern areas of Pakistan. In both regions, many farmers make a good profit from growing the poppies from which opium is processed. Raising the opium poppy was legal until 1979, when the new government, led by General Zia, cracked down and declared that the production and use of any stimulants was against Islamic law.

Until about 1995, the Southeast Asian country of Burma was the leading producer of opium. During the mid-1990s,

Afghanistan surpassed Burma, raising and exporting 2,200 to 2,400 metric tons of opium per year. Opium sales supported the Taliban regime in Afghanistan, but neighboring Pakistan must take some blame in the matter.

Beginning in 1993, Pakistan's government cracked down on the production and sale of opium. The program was a considerable success. Farmers in the Northwest Frontier Province were trained to grow different crops, and opium production fell by about 90 percent. This dramatic success was balanced by a new problem, however: opium and heroin consumption.

The Taliban government in Afghanistan depended completely on the sale of opium. The Taliban sent great amounts of opium into and through Pakistan. Sections of the Baluchistan Desert, which once saw mostly camels bearing wool and cotton, now witness high-speed trucks carrying opium and heroin. The drugs are taken to the Mahkran coast and shipped to drug markets in the major cities of Europe and North America. High-level Pakistani officials have been caught transferring drugs. In 1986, an army major was caught bringing 220 kilograms (485 pounds) of high-grade heroin from Karachi to Peshawar. The street value of that heroin was about $600 million in U.S. currency—almost equivalent to the entire U.S. foreign aid package to Pakistan that year!

Worst of all has been the increased drug use by Pakistanis. Government documents report that there were virtually no heroin addicts in Pakistan in 1979. The number of addicts rose to about 150,000 in 1985, and by 1999, the number had reached about 5 million people. If these figures are correct, it is safe to say that drug use, along with Islamic extremism, has become one of the major dangers facing Pakistan.

INTERNATIONAL TRADE

Legal trade with foreign countries—as opposed to the illegal traffic in drugs—has been a major element of Pakistan's economy over the past 50 years, bringing in large sums of money. The

In recent years, U.S. corporations have made their presence felt in Pakistan—the United States is the third-leading importer of goods to Pakistan. Pictured here are Muslim schoolgirls standing in front of a promotional sign for Pepsi in Karachi.

country's major export trade partners are the United States, United Arab Emirates, United Kingdom, and Germany. Saudi Arabia, United Arab Emirates, the United States, China, and Japan are the countries that import the most goods.

Pakistan's trade suffered between 1996 and 2001, when the Taliban ruled Afghanistan. During that period, trade in illegal goods soared, while legal trade was stagnant or declined. The cost to Pakistan's economy has been estimated by Ahmed Rashid: "Industry and trade became increasingly financed by laundered drug money and the black economy, which accounted for between 30 and 50 per cent of the total Pakistan economy."

PAKISTANIS ABROAD

One final ingredient has to be added into the economic formula: Pakistanis who work abroad. Pakistan's economy was

Although agriculture, industry, and service employ the most people in Pakistan, there is also an underground economy made up of money launderers and drug smugglers. Currency dealers, such as this man who is counting money in the city of Peshawar, near the Khyber Pass, often transfer millions of dollars in illegal funds to other cities throughout the world each day.

robust enough during the 1960s that most Pakistanis chose to stay home and work in the growing industries. After cutbacks in U.S. foreign aid during the 1970s, a boom in oil prices led many Pakistanis to move temporarily to Saudi Arabia, Kuwait, and the United Arab Emirates (U.A.E.) to work in the oil industry. Perhaps 2 million Pakistanis now live abroad in Arab nations, and as many as 5 million Pakistanis live in Europe and the United States. Even if they become citizens of the countries in which they live, most Pakistanis abroad retain a deep loyalty to their homeland. And the money they send back is definitely important to the economy of Pakistan.

In sum, Pakistan has a hybrid economy, one based on an almost equal division between agriculture, industry, and service. However, its economy is fragile, both because of physical geographical considerations such as soil salinization, and geopolitical factors such as the proximity of Afghanistan and conflicts over oil pipelines. In addition, the fragility of the economy supports illicit activities, such as drug smuggling and money laundering. What Pakistan's economy lacks most is coherent management. The Pakistanis are a hardworking, proud people who want to succeed in the capitalist world, but the landscape and environment they have inherited is better suited to a combination of a free-market and government management.

To the extent that any Third World nation can become a developed country, Pakistan has that opportunity. However, the country will remain on the verge of disaster as long as its population growth continues at the current rate.

Living in Pakistan Today

Many people in Pakistan today identify themselves first as Muslims, second as tribal or clan members, and third as Pakistanis. As author Stephen Alter wrote in his 2001 book, *Amritsar to Lahore: A Journey Across the India-Pakistan Border:* "Patriotic sentiments dictate that if you are one thing—a citizen of Pakistan, for instance, or a citizen of India—you cannot be the other. This sense of exclusivity and opposition has made it difficult for Pakistan to form its own distinct identity. There is no doubt in the minds of most Pakistanis that they are not Indians, but still the larger question, 'Who am I?' remains unanswered." This does not mean that Pakistanis are unpatriotic. Many Pakistanis fervently wave their flag and exclaim, "*Hum hain Pakistani! Hum Jitengey! Hum Jitengey!* " ("We are Pakistani! We will win! We will win!"). As Stephen Alter puts it, though, the question for many Pakistanis remains: "Who am I?"

All regional studies tend to come up with composite examples of what people's lives are like. Perhaps a better appreciation of what Pakistanis want from themselves and their country can be gained from a study of people who are heroes to present-day Pakistanis.

The first hero of Pakistan was Muhammad Ali Jinnah, who died in 1948. Much as they revere Jinnah's memory, few Pakistanis today can remember much about him, since he died nearly 60 years ago. No Pakistani leader since Jinnah has evoked the same type of admiration; even the Bhuttos had as many critics as they had supporters. Therefore, Pakistanis have found a series of folk heroes, who give some idea of what it means to be Pakistani.

ABDUL SATTAR EDHI

Religious beliefs require Muslims to give charity to the poor. The recognized amount is 2.5 percent of a person's yearly income. Some Pakistanis go much further: They are leaders of humanitarian efforts.

Abdul Sattar Edhi is one of the most instantly recognizable heroes of Pakistan and many consider him to be one of the most active philanthropists in the world. Born in Gujarat in 1931, Edhi spent years of his youth caring for his mother, who suffered from both paralysis and mental illness. He moved to Pakistan at the time of the partition and immediately established the Edhi Foundation. He then set up a free medical treatment center and a trust fund to support an ambulance service.

That was only the beginning. Edhi went on to create 13 free homes for unwanted or abandoned babies. About 6,000 people live in these homes today. He also developed the world's largest volunteer ambulance service, which is known for its 24-hour service and its prompt response to accidents. There are also animal shelters and a pilot program of posts for the aid of accident victims along Pakistan's highways. In recognition of his philanthropic endeavors, Edhi was presented with the Ramon

Magsaysay Award in 1986 (along with his wife, Begum Bilquis Edhi, who heads the Bilquis Edhi Foundation); the International Balzan Prize for Humanity, Peace and Brotherhood in 2000; and the Life Time Achievement Award by the World Memon Organisation (WMO) in 2005. In the future, Edhi plans to construct hospitals throughout Pakistan.

IMRAN KHAN

A second folk hero, of a very different type, is Imran Khan. Born in 1952, Khan attended school in Lahore, then went to England to study at Oxford's Keble College. There, he became a star cricket player, serving as Oxford's team captain in 1974. Khan then returned to Pakistan and became captain of the national cricket team. He served between 1982–1983, 1985–1987, and 1988–1992. In 1992, Khan led the team to victory over the British in the World Cup finals held in Melbourne, Australia.

Khan was a household name in Pakistan for the rest of the decade. Known as the world's most eligible bachelor, he remained a playboy until 1995, when he married Jemima Goldsmith, daughter of a British multimillionaire. Jemima converted to Islam and took the new name "Haiqa." She adapted to Pakistani life, wearing traditional clothing and becoming actively involved in charity work. She and Khan have two children, but the couple divorced in 2004.

Soon after his retirement from playing cricket in 1992, Khan experienced a personal return to Islam. Rejoicing in his newfound faith, Khan decided to enter politics. Pakistani disillusionment with the government had reached an all-time high in the mid- and late 1990s. The reforms promised by Benazir Bhutto had not come about, and Pakistanis felt that in many ways, they were worse off than they had been a generation before. Khan formed a new party, the *Tehrik-e-Insaaf*, and announced his candidacy for prime minister. He ran a spirited, though flawed campaign. Khan got off to a bad start when an American woman accused him of fathering her four-year-old

Imran Khan, the former captain of the national cricket team, helped Pakistan capture the inaugural International Cricket Council World Cup in 1992. After his playing days, Khan entered politics and is today a member of Pakistan's parliament.

daughter, a charge Khan denied. For a few weeks in January 1997, the overseas Pakistani press, especially the six Bengali-language newspapers in New York City, had a field day with the rumors and speculations.

Khan continued his campaign, but lost in the February election. He and his followers did not win a single seat in parliament (the legislature). Khan may have failed in part because Pakistani election law allows the right to vote only after age 21.

Many of his admirers were much younger. In October 2002, Khan was elected to represent the Mianwali District, in southern Punjab, as a member of parliament.

NUSRAT FATEH ALI KHAN

A third folk hero, perhaps the best-known Pakistani of the last 20 years, is Nusrat Fateh Ali Khan. Born in Faisalbad in 1948, Khan came from a family that had provided *qawwali* singers for more than 600 years. Qawwali are devotional songs, based on poetry.

Khan originally intended to become a physician, but he eavesdropped on his father's singing classes and then studied with him. Khan's first public performance was at his father's funeral in 1964. He then sang with his father's two brothers, and after the death of one of his uncles in 1971, he became the leader of the family. His fame spread throughout Pakistan during the 1970s, and then throughout the world in the following decade.

He first performed in England in 1985, where he formed an important friendship with rock singer Peter Gabriel. The two men collaborated on the soundtrack to the controversial film *The Last Temptation of Christ* in 1988. Peter Gabriel's label began to produce albums of Khan's songs.

Khan's health began to fail in the 1990s. Like many Western opera singers, he was extremely overweight and suffered from liver problems. Nevertheless, he continued to perform to sold-out audiences at New York's Radio City Music Hall as late as 1996. Khan died in 1997, leaving millions of fans from around the world stunned. His nephew, Rahat Nusrat Fateh Ali Khan, became his successor. He has already performed around the world, including at the Hollywood Bowl and in New York City's Central Park.

MUHAMMAD ABDUR RAHMAN CHUGHTAI

Muhammad Abdur Rahman Chughtai is a fourth important Pakistani folk hero. Born in Lahore in 1889, Chughtai started his education at a mosque in Lahore, then went on to study art at home and abroad.

Chughtai was steeped in Mughal and Muslim tradition, but he looked to the West for some of his inspiration. Watercolors and etchings were known in Pakistan only as imported art forms until Chughtai began to mold them into styles that honored earlier Mughal works. Perhaps most important, Chughtai introduced portraiture to Pakistan. Muslims believe that any direct representation of the Prophet Muhammad or of Allah are idolatry, and portrait painting never flourished until Chughtai's work became known. He made portraiture respectable in Pakistan.

Pakistanis are most familiar with Chughtai's engravings, but his watercolors are better known abroad. It is said that Queen Elizabeth II has eight Chughtai watercolors in her private collection. Other Chughtai works have been part of numerous exhibitions outside of Pakistan.

Chughtai died at his birthplace in Lahore in 1975. His son completed a new museum of his father's works in 2000.

THE ROLE OF WOMEN

No women are included in this list of Pakistani folk heroes. This is not meant to suggest that there are no heroines in modern-day Pakistan. Rather, the lack of women suggests that since the late 1970s, when General Zia proclaimed a return to traditional Islamic law, women have been increasingly cloistered in Pakistani society. Women are expected to play a secondary, supporting role to their husbands. The distinction between the sexes, drawn at birth, was described by journalist Jan Goodwin:

> The delivery of a baby boy is greeted with felicitations, parties, and, in some Muslim countries, even celebratory bursts of gunfire. The birth of a girl, on the other hand, is invariably a time for mourning. Even in every-day speech in much of the Arab world, when a silence falls at a gathering, the phrase uttered is Yat Bint, "a girl is born."

In Pakistan, the birth of a girl is often seen as bad fortune, because they do not add anything to a family's wealth. Pakistani society continues to be very conservative and girls such as the one pictured here do not have the same opportunities as their male counterparts.

And when one is, midwives have been known to abandon a delivery the moment they realize the child they have just helped into the world is of the "wrong" sex.

In Pakistan, and in much of the Third World, the birth of a girl is seen as bad fortune, because she will eventually leave her family home and become part of the "wealth" of her husband's family. Because of this perceived loss, many Pakistani families do much less for female children than male ones. Boys and girls receive different treatment in everything from schooling to clothing, and even to food.

There was a period, between about 1960 and 1980, when young Pakistani women were given more opportunities for growth and advancement. Many middle-aged women in Pakistan remember this as a time of glorious possibility. For nearly all women born after 1980, however, the future seems grim. Pakistan has reverted to a traditional, fundamentalist code for the genders.

THE PAKISTANI PEOPLE

As the aforementioned list of folk heroes suggests, Pakistanis are an enthusiastic and emotional people. Although the British Raj endured for just over a century, it left some important imprints on Pakistan. This can be seen in the excitement over sports such as cricket and the desire to send musical geniuses such as Nusrat Fateh Ali Khan abroad to win international recognition. Pakistanis are talkative people, who often ask questions that some outsiders find embarrassing. Writer Stephen Alter recounted several episodes in which he was bombarded with questions before he even got to know the questioner. One of these conversations indicated both the eager nature of Pakistanis and how much they know about American culture:

> Immediately I saw a young boy running toward me. He was eight or nine years old and grabbed my hand in excitement.
>
> "Are you American?" he asked, in Urdu.
>
> When I nodded he seemed delighted.
>
> "Then you must have seen a farishta," he said. "Tell me what they're like."

Farishta is the word for angel, but his question still puzzled me.

"What do you mean?" I asked.

"You know, the farishta you have in your country," said the boy, insistently. "Haven't you seen them?"

By this time five or six other children had gathered around me, all of them about the same age.

"I'm sorry, I don't know what you mean," I said. "What kind of farishta?"

The boy and his friends looked up at me impatiently. "You know, the ones we see on TV."

The children then struck a pose that showed Alter they were referring to the superheroes of an American show. Even a country such as Pakistan, which prides itself on being one of the largest and the most cohesive Muslim nations in the world, is not immune to the attractions of American music and television programs.

9

Pakistan
Looks Ahead

In Muhammad Iqbal's poem "Two Planets," he writes:

> Two planets meeting face to face. One to the other cried "How
> sweet If endlessly we might embrace, And here for ever stay!
> how sweet If Heaven a little might relent, And leave our light
> in one light blent!" But through that longing to dissolve In
> one, the parting summons sounded. Immutably the stars
> revolve, By changeless orbits each is bounded; Eternal union
> is a dream, And severance the world's law supreme.

It is impossible to say whether Muhammad Iqbal's poem referred
to the time-honored tradition of star-crossed lovers, to the law of
physics, or to the factors that separate nations and peoples from one
another. Perhaps he meant all of the above in this poem.

When India was partitioned in 1947, the region of Kashmir was also divided between India and Pakistan and many Kashmiris were separated from their relatives. Pictured here is a Kashmiri girl reading a letter from her relatives who live on the other side of the Neelum River, in Indian Kashmir.

If Iqbal's poem is interpreted in a geopolitical manner, then it might be said that he was a prophet as well as a poet. This poem could be used to describe the dilemmas faced by Pakistan and India in the twentieth and twenty-first centuries.

Iqbal's poem brings to mind the many factors that lead toward separation and disunion within Pakistan. Iqbal died in 1938, but even now, in the early years of the twenty-first century, the kind of questions he asked are still relevant: Will Pakistan endure? Will its people be content? Will the pressing problems of population growth and poverty be overcome?

The dangers that Pakistan confronts are numerous. Population growth remains the main dilemma. Pakistan has the world's sixth-largest population with 166 million people and will likely pass Brazil to move into fifth place sometime around 2020. Karachi has become one of the world's largest cities, with more than its share of drugs, poverty, and crime. The division between rich and poor continues to widen. Then, looming above all the other problems is the seemingly unsolvable conflict with India.

Whether the tensions could be brought to an end if the two countries came to an agreement over Kashmir is uncertain. The Indian-Pakistani conflict runs deep; it is rooted in the migration of Hindus to India and Muslims to Pakistan in 1947. These moves left millions of people uprooted. Numerous people on both sides of the border have never met their relatives on the other side. This division by borders might be overcome if there was goodwill between the two governments, but such goodwill does not exist. In fact, some journalists believe the two governments actually fuel the border tensions in order to control dissent in their home populations. Whether or not this is true, there is no doubt the situation has grown more serious since May 1998, when both nations tested nuclear devices.

The situation is unlike the cold war that was waged between the United States and Soviet Union during the second half of the twentieth century. The two superpowers did not share borders, except for some icy islands in the Bering Strait. Even though their rivalry was intense and occurred on a worldwide stage, there was no religious dimension to their conflict. By contrast, Pakistan and India have a feud that is economic, political, and religious.

Recent studies estimate that at least 100 million people combined would die on the two sides if there was a nuclear exchange on the subcontinent. That would only be from the explosion of bombs. The ensuing fallout would also poison the environment of hundreds of millions of other people who lived in the region. For these reasons, a nuclear exchange must be prevented.

History tells us that a people and a nation cannot endure if they are split apart from each other. It may, therefore, have been a blessing in disguise when East Pakistan went its own way in 1971 to become Bangladesh. By doing so, Bangladesh paved the way for West Pakistan to become a more unified nation-state.

Geography shows us that centripetal and centrifugal forces are constantly at odds in nation-states. This can be illustrated in the case of the United States. Although the Civil War (1861–1865) ended most attempts at outright separation, there are many aspects of American life that still divide people. The geographer and sociologist Joel Garreau claimed in 1981 that there were nine nations of North America, not one. Garreau identified the following "nations": Quebec, New England, the Foundry, Dixie, Mexamerica, Ectopia, the Islands, the Empty Quarter, and the Breadbasket.

The history of religion demonstrates that spiritual leaders and different faiths have thrived on the Indian subcontinent. Religious plurality, rather than religious oneness, has been the norm in South Asia, but it is uncertain whether religious plurality will return to Pakistan. Today, it is the land of the pure, a land for Muslims in a sea of Hindus and Christians.

Political history suggests that Pakistan has a rough road ahead. The very concept of nation-state is in some trouble in the twenty-first century. Inventions such as the Internet, cellular phones, and other means of communication have the potential to undermine the fierce adherence to nationalism of the nineteenth and early twentieth centuries. For a country such as the United States—which has practiced democracy for 200 years—or for one like Iceland—which has a remarkably homogeneous population—the twenty-first century may not be so threatening. For a country such as Pakistan, however, created in 1947, and developed amid strife and conflict, it is possible that the system so painfully built by Muhammad Ali Jinnah could easily come apart.

This is especially possible in Pakistan because of the long-held tendency toward tribalism. The Pashtuns, for example, live as independently as possible from the national government, and have as much affinity with their fellow Pashtuns on the Afghan side of the border as with other Pakistanis.

This, however, does not mean Pakistan cannot survive. Pakistan may defy the odds and endure. It may even thrive. All that can be said with certainty is that the country has surmounted many challenges in the last 50 years, and it will likely face many more in the future.

Physical Geography

Location Southern Asia, bordering the Arabian Sea, between India on the east and Iran and Afghanistan on the west and China in the north

Area Total: 310,409 square miles (803,940 square kilometers); *land*: 300,671 square miles (778,720 square kilometers); *water:* 9,738 square miles (25,220 square kilometers)—about the size of France and the United Kingdom combined

Climate and Ecosystem Mostly hot, dry desert; temperate in northwest; arctic in north

Terrain Flat Indus plain in east; mountains in north and northwest; Baluchistan Plateau in west

Elevation Extremes Lowest point is Indian Ocean, sea level; highest point is K2 (Mount Godwin-Austen) 28,251 feet (8,611 meters)

Land Use Arable land, 24.44%; permanent crops, 0.84%; other, 74.72% (2005)

Irrigated Land 70,388 square miles (182,300 square kilometers) (2003)

Natural Hazards Frequent earthquakes, occasionally severe especially in north and west; flooding along the Indus after heavy rains (July and August)

Environmental Issues Water pollution from raw sewage, industrial wastes, and agricultural runoff; limited natural freshwater resources; a majority of the population does not have access to potable water; deforestation; soil erosion; desertification

People

Population 165,803,560 (July 2006 est.); males, 84,763,791 (2006 est.); females, 81,039,769 (July 2006 est.)

Population Density 177 people per square kilometer

Population Growth Rate 2.09% (2006 est.)

Net Migration Rate -0.59 migrant(s)/1,000 population (2006 est.)

Fertility Rate 4 children born/woman (2006 est.)

Life Expectancy at Birth Total population: 63.39 years; male, 62.4 years; female, 64.44 years (2006 est.)

Median Age Total Population: 19.8 years; male, 19.7 years; female, 20 years

97

Ethnic Groups	Punjabi, Sindhi, Pashtun (Pathan), Baloch, Muhajir (immigrants from India at the time of partition and their descendants)
Religions	Muslim, 97% (Sunni, 77%; Shia, 20%); Christian, Hindu, and other, 3%
Literacy	(Age 15 and over can read and write) Total population: 48.7%; male, 61.7%; female, 35.2% (1999 est.)

Economy

Currency	Pakistani rupee (PKR)
GDP Purchasing Power Parity (PPP)	$384.9 billion (2005 est.)
GDP Per Capita (PPP)	$2,400 (2005 est.)
Labor Force	46.84 million (2005 est.)
Unemployment	6.6% plus substantial underemployment (2005 est.)
Labor Force by Occupation	Agriculture, 42%; industry, 20%; services, 38% (1996 est.)
Industries	Textiles and apparel, food processing, pharmaceuticals, construction materials, paper products, fertilizer, shrimp
Exports	$14.85 billion (2005 est.)
Imports	$21.26 billion (2005 est.)
Leading Trade Partners	*Exports*: U.S., 23.5%; UAE, 7.4%; UK, 7.3%; Germany, 5%; Hong Kong, 4.4% (2004); *Imports*: Saudi Arabia, 11.6%; UAE, 10%; U.S., 9.7%; China, 8.4%; Japan, 6.5%; Kuwait, 5.6% (2004)
Export Commodities	Textiles (garments, bed linen, cotton cloth, yarn), rice, leather goods, sports goods, chemicals, manufactures, carpets and rugs
Import Commodities	Petroleum, petroleum products, machinery, plastics, transportation equipment, edible oils, paper and paperboard, iron and steel, tea
Transportation	*Roadways*: total, 158,090 miles (254,410 kilometers); paved, 94,854 miles (152,646 kilometers, including 367 kilometers of expressways); unpaved, 63,236 miles (101,764 kilometers) (2003); *Airports:* 134–91 paved (2005); *Railways*: 5,073 miles (8,163 kilometers)

Government

Country Name	Conventional long form: Islamic Republic of Pakistan; Conventional short form: Pakistan; Former: West Pakistan

Capital City	Islamabad
Type of Government	Federal Republic
Head of Government	Prime Minister Shaukat Aziz (since August 28, 2004)
Chief of State	President General Pervez Musharraf (since June 20, 2001)
Independence	August 14, 1947 (from Great Britain)
Administrative Divisions	Provinces, 1 territory, and 1 capital territory

Communications

TV Stations	22 (plus seven low-power repeaters) (1997)
Phones	(including cellular): 9,525,100 (2004)
Internet Users	7.5 million (2005)

* Source: *CIA-The World Factbook* (2006)

2500 B.C.	Civilization appears in the Indus River valley; many of its cities are noteworthy for their sophisticated planning and irrigation.
1700 B.C.	The Indus River cities disappear.
1600–600 B.C.	Known as the Aryan or Vedic period; the Aryans are a group of Central Asian tribes that enter the subcontinent and come to dominate Pakistan and northern India.
326 B.C.	Alexander the Great arrives on the Indus; in the Punjab he fights a battle against King Porus; the Greek army floats down the Indus River, then splits into two groups—one returns to Mesopotamia by sea; the other, under Alexander, marches across Baluchistan.
A.D. 711	A Muslim army invades Sind from the Arabian Sea; this is the beginning of the introduction of Islam to the subcontinent.
1526	Babur, a Turco-Mongol, invades the subcontinent and founds the Mughal Empire.
1526–1760	The Mughal Empire rules northern India and Pakistan.
1757	Robert Clive helps Great Britain win the Battle of Plassey; the interests of the East India Company become paramount on the subcontinent.
1857	The Great Indian Mutiny takes place; Great Britain subdues the Hindu Revolt with difficulty; India is placed under the direct rule of Queen Victoria, and the subcontinent is called the British Raj.
1869	Mohandas Gandhi born in Porbandar, India.
1876	Muhammad Ali Jinnah born in Karachi.
1877	Muhammad Iqbal born in Sialkot, Punjab.
1889	Muhammad Abdur Rahman Chughtai born in Lahore.
1933	At Cambridge, England, a group of students from India invent the word Pakistan, which is drawn from P (Punjab), A (Afghan), K (Kashmir), and stan (Baluchistan).
1939	A group of German mountain climbers sets out for Nanga Parbat, in northern Pakistan; they are taken prisoner by the British at the beginning of World War II.

1947	Lord Louis Mountbatten arrives as the last British viceroy; the British withdraw and the subcontinent is divided into two countries: Pakistan and India; Pakistan is further divided into East and West Pakistan.
1948	Muhammad Ali Jinnah dies.
1952	Imran Khan born in Lahore.
1953	Climbers reach the top of both Mount Everest and Nanga Parbat.
1956	The country is renamed the Islamic Republic of Pakistan.
1960	Pakistan and India sign the Indus Waters Treaty.
1968	Work begins on the Tarbela Dam in northern Pakistan.
1971	East Pakistan breaks away and declares itself the new country of Bangladesh.
1973	A new Pakistani constitution is approved; it provides for a president, prime minister, and bicameral parliament.
1977	Zulfikar Bhutto is put in prison.
1979	Zulfikar Bhutto is executed; opium cultivation is prohibited; Soviet Union invades Afghanistan.
1980–1988	The Afghan resistance fighters are assisted by arms, ammunition, and technical advice from many nations, including the United States and Pakistan.
1986	Benazir Bhutto comes home to Pakistan.
1988	Muhammad Zia-ul-Haq dies in a plane crash; Benazir Bhutto becomes prime minister.
1992	Pakistan wins the World Cup in cricket.
1997	Nusrat Fateh ali Khan dies; Imran Khan runs for Prime Minister.
1998	India and Pakistan detonate their first nuclear bombs.
1999	General Pervez Musharraf seizes power in a three-hour coup; he appoints an eight-member National Security Council and suspends the constitution until he sorts out Pakistan's economic problems.
2001	Under Musharraf, Pakistan aligns itself with the United States in the war on international terrorism.
2002	Musharraf transfers executive powers to Prime Minister Zafarullah Khan Jamali.
2004	Former Finance Minster Shaukat Aziz elected prime minister.
2005	Pakistan is rocked by a 7.6 earthquake northeast of Islamabad.

Bibliography

Ahmad, Kazi S. *A Geography of Pakistan.* New York: Oxford University Press, 1964.

Ahmed, Akbar S. *Jinnah, Pakistan and Islamic Identity: The Search for Saladin.* New York: Routledge, 1997.

Alter, Stephen. *Amritsar to Lahore: A Journey Across the India-Pakistan Border.* Philadelphia, Pa.: University of Pennsylvania Press, 2001.

Bhutto, Benazir. *Daughter of Destiny.* New York: Simon and Schuster, 1989.

Bose, Sumantra. *Kashmir: Roots of Conflict, Paths to Peace.* Cambridge, Mass.: Harvard University Press, 2003.

Burton, Richard F. *Sindh And the Races that Inhabit the Valley of the Indus.* London, 1851.

Cohen, Stephen Philip. *The Idea of Pakistan.* Washington, D.C.: Brookings Institution Press, 2004.

Fairley, Jean. *The Lion River: The Indus.* The John Day Company, 1975.

Garreau, Joel. *The Nine Nations of North America.* New York: Avon Books, 1981.

Goodwin, Jan. *Price of Honor: Muslim Women Lift the Veil of Silence on the Islamic World.* New York: Plume-Penguin, 1994.

Haqqani, Husain. *Pakistan: Between Mosque and Military.* Washington, D.C.: Carnegie Endowment for International Peace, 2005.

Husain, Ishrat. *Pakistan: The Economy of an Elitist State.* New York: Oxford University Press, 1999.

Kiernan, V.G., trans. and ed. *Poems from Iqbal.* London: John Murray, 1955.

King, John, Bradley Mayhew, and David St. Vincent. *Pakistan.* Oakland, Calif.: Lonely Planet Publications, 1998.

Kipling, Rudyard. *Kim.* New York: Macmillan, 1901.

Kux, Dennis. *Pakistan: Flawed not Failed State.* New York: The Foreign Policy Association, 2001.

Margolis, Eric S. *War at the Top of the World: The Struggle for Afghanistan, Kashmir, and Tibet.* New York: Routledge, 2000.

Mittal, Anuradha. "On the True Cause of World Hunger," an interview by Derrick Jensen. *The Sun.* February 2002.

Ptolemy, Claudius. *The Geography.* Edward Luther Stevenson, trans. and ed. Mineola, N.Y.: Dover Publications, 1991.

Ramana, M.V., and A. H. Nayyar. "India, Pakistan and the Bomb." *ScientificAmerican,* Vol. 285, no. 6. December 2001: 72–83.

Rashid, Ahmed. *Taliban: Militant Islam, Oil and Fundamentalism in Central Asia.* New Haven, Conn.: Yale University Press, 2000.

Robertson, Sir George Scott. *K.C.S.I. The Kafirs of the Hindu-Kush.* London, 1900.

Toynbee, Arnold J. *Between Oxus and Jumnai.* New York: Oxford University Press, 1961.

White, Peter T., and Steve Raymer. "The Poppy—For Good and Evil." *National Geographic.* February 1985: 143–188.

Further Reading

Ahmed, Akbar S., and Ahmed Akbar. *Jinnah, Pakistan and Islamic Identity: The Search for Saladin.* New York: Routledge, 1997.

Ganguly, Sumit. *Conflict Unending?: India-Pakistan Tensions Since 1947.* New York: Columbia University Press, 2002.

Goodwin, William. *Pakistan* (Modern Nations of the World). San Diego, Calif.: Lucent Books, 2002.

Haque, Jameel. *Pakistan* (Countries of the World). Milwaukee, Wisc.: Gareth Stevens, 2002.

Jaffrelot, Christophe, ed. *Pakistan: Nationalism Without a Nation?* London: Zed Books, 2002.

Sheehan, Sean. *Pakistan* (Cultures of the World). New York: Benchmark Books, 1996.

Web sites

South Asia: A Global Perspective
http://www.cet.edu/earthinfo/sasia/SAmain.html

CIA World Factbook—Pakistan
http://www.cia.gov/cia/publications/factbook/geos/pk.html

The Economist Country Briefing: Pakistan
http://www.economist.com/countries/Pakistan/

The Ancient Indus Valley
http://www.harappa.com/har/har0.html

Pakistan: A Country Study
http://lcweb2.loc.gov/frd/cs/pktoc.html

Kashmir: The Origins of the Dispute
http://news.bbc.co.uk/2/hi/south_asia/1762146.stm

Pakistan Today—Source for News on South Asia
http://www.paktoday.com/

Index

106

Index

Picture Credits

page:

SAMUEL WILLARD CROMPTON is the author or editor of 40 books, many of them written for Chelsea House. He is also an adjunct professor of history at Holyoke Community College and Westfield State College, both in Massachusetts.

Series Editor **CHARLES F. GRITZNER** is distinguished professor of geography at South Dakota State University in Brookings. He is now in his fifth decade of college teaching, research, and writing. In addition to teaching, he enjoys writing, working with teachers, and sharing his love of geography with readers. As the series editor for Chelsea House's MODERN WORLD CULTURES and MODERN WORLD NATIONS series, he has a wonderful opportunity to combine each of these hobbies. Gritzner has served as both president and executive director of the National Council for Geographic Education and has received the Council's highest honor, the George J. Miller Award for Distinguished Service to Geographic Education.